RSPB EVERYDAY
GUIDE TO BRITISH WILDLIFE

BLOOMSBURY WILDLIFE
LONDON · OXFORD · NEW YORK · NEW DELHI · SYDNEY

For Nicky

BLOOMSBURY WILDLIFE
Bloomsbury Publishing Plc,
50 Bedford Square, London, WC1B 3DP, UK
Bloomsbury Publishing Ireland Limited,
29 Earlsfort Terrace, Dublin 2, D02 AY28, Ireland

BLOOMSBURY, BLOOMSBURY WILDLIFE and the Diana logo are trademarks of
Bloomsbury Publishing Plc

First published in the United Kingdom 2025

Copyright © Charlie Elder 2025
Photos © 2025 as credited on pages 205–206

Charlie Elder has asserted his right under the Copyright, Designs and Patents Act, 1988,
to be identified as Author of this work

All rights reserved. No part of this publication may be: i) reproduced or transmitted in any form,
electronic or mechanical, including photocopying, recording or by means of any information storage or
retrieval system without prior permission in writing from the publishers; or ii) used or reproduced in any way
for the training, development or operation of artificial intelligence (AI) technologies, including generative
AI technologies. The rights holders expressly reserve this publication from the text and data mining
exception as per Article 4(3) of the Digital Single Market Directive (EU) 2019/790

Bloomsbury Publishing Plc does not have any control over, or responsibility for, any third-party
websites referred to or in this book. All internet addresses given in this book were correct at the time
of going to press. The author and publisher regret any inconvenience caused if addresses have changed
or sites have ceased to exist, but can accept no responsibility for any such changes

A catalogue record for this book is available from the British Library

Library of Congress Cataloguing-in-Publication data has been applied for

ISBN: PB: 978-1-3994-1332-9
ePub: 978-1-3994-1333-6
ePDF: 978-1-3994-1334-3

2 4 6 8 10 9 7 5 3 1

Designed by Austin Taylor
Printed and bound in China by C&C Offset Printing Co. Ltd, Shenzhen, Guangdong

To find out more about our authors and books visit www.bloomsbury.com
and sign up for our newsletters
For product safety related questions contact productsafety@bloomsbury.com

Published under licence from RSPB Sales Limited to raise awareness of the RSPB
(charity registration in England and Wales no 207076 and Scotland no SC037654).

For all licensed products sold by Bloomsbury Publishing Limited, Bloomsbury Publishing
Limited will donate a minimum of 2% from all sales to RSPB Sales Ltd, which gives all of
its distributable profits through Gift Aid to the RSPB.

Contents

Introduction 4

Mammals 6
Reptiles and amphibians 44
Garden ponds 52
Butterflies 62
Gardening for butterflies 74
Moths 88
Caterpillar defences 108
Dragonflies and damselflies 110
Beetles and bugs 124
Bees, wasps and flies 140
Wild ways to boost biodiversity 150
Other invertebrates 158
Fish 168
Other coastal wildlife 180
Rockpools 184
Along the coast 190
Strandline finds 200
Conserving British nature 202
Further reading 204
Photograph credits 205
Index 207

Introduction

From a beetle larva that hitches a ride on bees to a moth bearing the face of a reputed witch; from a caterpillar that mimics a snake to a fish that likes to sunbathe; from a carnivore that lines its nest with the fur of its prey to a fly whose life cycle has provided vital clues in murder investigations ... the British Isles are home to an array of fascinating wildlife.

Varied habitats – from woodlands and grasslands to uplands, heathlands and wetlands – and a lengthy coastline sustain a wealth of animals. Among them are more than 100 species of land and marine mammal; dozens of butterfly, dragonfly and bumblebee species; around 2,500 species of moth, and more than 4,000 species of beetle.

In exploring the rich diversity of our fauna, this book does not seek to be comprehensive – and given there are more than 7,000 species of fly in Britain, that will come as a relief to many! Instead, the RSPB *Everyday Guide to British Wildlife* focuses on some of the most common, widespread and charismatic species that live in this country – helping the reader to identify and learn more about those they encounter. Nearly 400 species are referred to in the text, with helpful photographs highlighting important characteristics for the identification of everything from bats to bumblebees, dolphins to demoiselles, crabs to crickets and hawk-moths to hoverflies.

INTRODUCTION

As this is a companion title to the RSPB *Everyday Guide to British Birds*, this guide doesn't include our feathered friends, concentrating instead on the abundance of other species you can see in the British Isles. It's divided into ten sections: Mammals, Marine life, Reptiles and amphibians, Butterflies, Moths, Dragonflies and damselflies, Beetles and bugs, Bees, wasps and flies, Other invertebrates, and Fish.

Written for the general nature enthusiast, this guide dispenses with the restraints of strict taxonomy in order to display together some species based on appearance – making it easier for readers to find what they are looking for. In addition, we have presented some pairs of species that may easily be confused side by side to better illustrate their key differences. Identifying the species we can see when we spend time outdoors can help forge closer connections with the natural world. This guide will help you put a name to what you have spotted and describes the unique characteristics that make each species special. We've also included a number of double-page features on topics that will enhance your wildlife watching even more, such as how to create a pond or select garden plants for pollinators – simple ways to provide a home for nature at a time when many of our species have suffered worrying declines.

Above all, this book is a celebration of Britain's fauna and the wealth of wonderful animals, great and small, that we are fortunate to have on our doorstep.

Happy wildlife watching!

▲ *Clockwise from top left:* Common Hawker dragonflies, Grey Seal, Common Frog, Stoats, Three-spined Stickleback, Stag Beetle, Bank Vole, Red Deer stags.

Mammals

Hedgehog

The **Hedgehog** is a contender for the most popular and adored wild mammal in Britain – which is somewhat surprising given it is covered in spines.

You might have thought these podgy pin-cushions would be the least appealing of animals. Yet there is something undeniably cute about them. From their docile nature and rotund build to the dark snout, bright eyes and party trick of rolling up like a prickly pear when threatened, these nocturnal garden visitors have undeniable appeal.

The fact that this idiosyncratic insectivore, popularised by Beatrix Potter as Mrs Tiggy-Winkle, has won a place in our hearts has helped garner support for Hedgehog conservation – and they

▶ Hedgehogs eat a range of invertebrates, such as earthworms and beetles.

Garden visitors

Our back gardens can provide the perfect habitat for Hedgehogs, with dense vegetation and grassy areas. Fences block their movements, but gaps or specially cut holes (*left*) ensure these wanderers can get about freely. An opening 13cm by 13cm is sufficient for a Hedgehog to pass through, while too small for many pets.

Hedgehogs may rest up in long vegetation or hibernate under wood piles, so gardeners should take care when strimming or lighting bonfires. Avoiding pesticides will also ensure plenty of invertebrate food for them. Artificial Hedgehog houses are be located in shady and quiet areas o the garden, and a tunnel entrance means they can remain safely out of reach of predators such as badgers.

Hedgehogs readily eat food pu out for them, though only small amounts should be provided as a supplement to their natural diet. Special Hedgehog foods

need all the friends they can get. A victim of habitat changes and road collisions, we come across this species far less often these days, dead or alive.

In the past Hedgehogs were not so fondly regarded, their 'crimes' including the myth that they suckled milk from resting cows at night. Many were killed in the seventeenth and eighteenth centuries as 'vermin' – despite their appetite for plant pests benefitting farmers and gardeners.

While such persecution is behind us, the Hedgehog population in Britain has suffered a worse fate in recent decades as the effects of agricultural intensification, pesticide use and increased traffic, among other factors, have driven down numbers from an estimated 36 million in the 1950s to fewer than a million today. Suburban populations are faring better than those in rural areas.

Generally solitary and non-territorial, Hedgehogs may roam about a mile a night in search of food, sleeping by day in makeshift nests dotted around their home range. They eat a variety of invertebrates – such as earthworms, caterpillars, beetles and slugs – as well as eggs and carrion.

You can spot Hedgehogs at night by torchlight, rustling along hedgerows and borders as they forage. Hedgehogs active in the day are either

Hibernation

In the colder months, when food is in short supply, Hedgehogs hibernate, slowing their metabolism and falling into a torpor to save energy – a survival strategy shared with bats and dormice. They tuck themselves away, curled up in a nest of leaves in a sheltered spot, such as under a garden shed, compost heap or log pile. However, they become active during milder spells in winter.

Hedgehogs breed between April and September, though mainly in May and June. The female gives birth to a litter of 4–6 young. Those born in the autumn may lack sufficient time to put on the weight required to survive winter hibernation.

short of food or possibly unwell.

Adult Hedgehogs have roughly 5,000–6,000 spines – thick, hollow hairs of tough keratin. They live for 2–3 years on average, with the oldest recorded in Europe reaching 16.

re available, while meat-based dog or cat food is also suitable. Hedgehogs are lactose intolerant, so a saucer of milk will do them no good at all, and bread offers little nutritional value.

A telltale sign your garden is being visited by Hedgehogs is the presence of their droppings. Dark, cylindrical and a few centimetres long, they resemble black slugs on the lawn.

Fox

The **Fox** hardly needs any introduction, being one of our most recognisable wild mammals – a dashing and canny predator that lives by its wits and can be found across the British Isles in all kinds of habitats, rural and urban.

A character in children's stories, subject of folklore and focus of heated debate regarding country sports, the wily Fox is a prominent figure in our culture. Yet despite its familiarity, size and distinctive orangey-brown colouring, this slender canine often keeps out of view, generally going about its business in the quiet hours.

The Fox is hard to confuse with any other animal, both in appearance and behaviour. It has slim features, a narrow muzzle and easy gait. Most notable is its rusty-red fur, which can vary in tone, and it has a white chest, a long bushy tail and upright ears that are dark on the back. Superficially it resembles a lean medium-sized dog, but the watchful and wary Fox always has a spirit of the wild about it.

Foxes are social animals, with family groups sharing a territory. They dig dens – also known as 'earths' – but to save the effort they may take over an unoccupied Badger burrow or use the shelter provided under sheds and buildings. Young are born in the spring, a litter typically numbering 4–5 cubs, which are weaned after about a month.

Intelligent opportunists, Foxes hunt and scavenge a range of foods – everything from birds, eggs, rodents and carrion to fruit, invertebrates and the contents of rubbish bins. They will famously kill poultry if given the chance, along with game birds, and also prey on Rabbits.

Urban Fox

If you want decent views of Foxes, towns and cities are your best bet! Urban Foxes in the suburbs of conurbations such as London, Bristol or Bournemouth (the latter boasting a staggering density of 23 Foxes per square kilometre), are far more confident than their more elusive country cousins.

Foxes are adaptable animals and have exploited the many opportunities that urban and suburban areas offer – not only shelter and safety from

Foxes can be found in woodlands, wetlands, moorland, grasslands, farmland, gardens, scrub, industrial sites and coastal areas – they favour mixed habitats that offer cover and sources of food. They have good eyesight, acute hearing and a keen sense of smell.

Foxes can live for more than nine years in the wild, but many are killed by road traffic, poisoning and shooting. They can also suffer from a range of infections and parasites, including mange caused by irritating skin mites. Hunting Foxes with dogs was made illegal under the Hunting Act 2004.

Tracks and signs

Fox tracks consist of four-toed prints, with claw marks. They resemble those of a small dog, however a dog print has a larger rear 'palm'. The separation of toes in the narrow Fox footprint also means a cross can be drawn through the open central space without the diagonal lines touching any pads – which is not possible with a dog paw print.

Fox droppings are long and twisted and may contain fur, bits of bone or fruit pips, while their dens have a musky smell and food remains may be discarded outside the entrance. They mark their territories with urine, which has a recognisably pungent odour.

persecution, but also ready supplies of discarded food. They began to colonise British towns and cities from the 1930s onwards, taking advantage of the growth in suburbia with its large gardens and leafy lanes, and have thrived. Attempts to control their numbers in urban districts were unsuccessful and abandoned in the 1980s.

Feeding garden Foxes is prevalent in many urban areas, though those who do so are advised against trying to hand feed, as not all people appreciate being approached by confident and inquisitive individuals.

While mainly nocturnal, and active at dawn and dusk, Foxes can sometimes be spotted basking in sunny, sheltered spots during the day. At night their sounds give their presence away – the three barks of a dog Fox or, in winter during the mating season, the disturbing, almost human-like, scream of a female vixen.

Grey Squirrel

Bright-eyed and bushy-tailed, the **Grey Squirrel** has plenty of character. Active by day, this agile and energetic mammal can be surprisingly tame in urban areas, offering children and adults alike the chance to enjoy a close encounter with wildlife.

Of the two squirrel species present in Britain, the non-native Grey Squirrel is far more common than the native **Red Squirrel**, which was once widespread but is now mostly concentrated in Scotland, northern England and a few coniferous woodland enclaves.

The Grey Squirrel was imported from North America in the late 1800s and early 1900s and released onto estates and into the wild. This opportunist woodland inhabitant spread far and wide, despite attempts to control expanding numbers, and has become an established resident of deciduous woods, parks and leafy gardens. Its UK population is estimated at close to three million. Grey Squirrels are adept climbers, able to run head first down a tree trunk, and can be noisy as they scamper through the leaf litter. They are also vocal, making chattering noises and harsh scolding calls when agitated. Rival males chase females through the treetops in the winter in the hope of pairing up. During spring, females give birth in a drey to a litter of 2–4 young, and may have a second litter in early autumn.

While appreciated by many, Grey Squirrels are considered something of a pest by others, given the damage they cause to forestry and crops by stripping bark and eating buds, and the fact they take birds' eggs and nestlings. In addition, this invasive non-native coloniser has been implicated

Red or Grey?

We have two species of squirrel in the British Isles, the grey and the red. The introduced Grey Squirrel is the larger of the two. It has peppery-grey fur and a bushy tail that is lighter around the edges. However, it can also have rusty-reddish patches around its face and on its back, particularly in the summer when its fur coat is less dense. This may cause it to be confused with the slimmer and scarcer **Red Squirrel** (*left*).

While coat colour may vary, the Red Squirrel is generally a richer chestnut-red all over and has tufts of hair at the top of its ears (although these disappear in summer).

Once widespread and numbering in the millions, Red Squirrels have lost ground over the last century and the British population now stands at less than a couple of hundred thousand. They are confined to Scotland and parts of northern England (including the Lake

in the decline of the shy native Red Squirrel. The heftier Grey Squirrel dominates food sources and can carry a virus known as squirrel pox, a disease which is fatal among smaller Red Squirrels.

Grey Squirrels have few natural predators and are particularly bold in cities, parks and gardens where they are accustomed to people, often visiting bird tables for peanuts and seeds. In rural areas they may keep their distance, even clambering around a tree to hide on the opposite side in order to keep out of view.

Dreys

Squirrels nest in dreys – spherical constructions of twigs and leaves positioned high off the ground and often built in the fork of a branch close to the tree trunk. A drey looks similar to the nest of a bird such as a Magpie, but has a high number of leaves visible in the interwoven mass.

As squirrels do not hibernate, they need to put on fat reserves to see them through the winter. In the autumn, Grey Squirrels gorge on acorns and other tree seeds. They also stash supplies in tree holes or buried just beneath the surface of the ground.

District), Ireland and Wales, as well as some islands, such as the Isle of Wight and Brownsea Island off Dorset.

Red Squirrels tend to be most active early in the morning and before dusk. They may be heard scampering through the canopy in coniferous forests or spotted visiting bird tables for food.

The Grey Squirrel can have a rusty-orange tinge to its fur, while the Red Squirrel (*far left*) is a more uniform chestnut-red.

MAMMALS 13

Rabbit

With long ears, large eyes and a fluffy white cotton-tail, the **Rabbit** is a very familiar part of our national fauna, an endearing character in books and much-loved companion in our homes as a pet.

But the wild Rabbits that we are accustomed to, hopping along hedgerows and road verges, in meadows and scrub, on farmland, heaths and downland are, in fact, native to southern Europe. It is thought that Britain's countryside was bunny-free until Norman settlers brought them to our shores for their meat and fur, with the species becoming properly established from the twelfth century onwards. They were much valued as a source of food and pelts and kept in enclosures known as warrens – a term that also refers to their burrow systems. Place names today containing the word 'warren' reflect this past Rabbit farming industry.

Given that Rabbits breed like, well, Rabbits, numbers multiplied and spread beyond their enclosures across the wider countryside. The impact of their nibbling on crops and grassland meant that over time they came to be considered an agricultural pest. Their booming population, which topped 100 million, was eventually decimated when the fatal viral disease myxomatosis reached the British Isles in the 1950s, wiping out an estimated 99 per cent. Today numbers have rallied but fluctuate, as disease outbreaks wax and wane, and there are around 38 million wild Rabbits in the UK.

Rabbits are mainly active at night, dawn and dusk, though can be seen during the day – especially in summer. When feeding, they are always alert to danger and tend to stick close to cover and their burrows for safety. Their nibbling incisors nip off grass very low to the ground, and the short turf

Rabbit or hare?

Rabbits live in colonies and breed and shelter in burrows. Hares, on the other hand, are more solitary and live, raise young and sleep out in the open, resting in a shallow scrape in the ground called a 'form'. They are animals of open ground, such as farmland and grassland. During the breeding season female hares fend off pursuing males by rearing up and boxing them – hence the expression 'Mad as a March hare'.

An adult **Brown Hare** (*left*) is larger than a Rabbit and has lengthy black-tipped ears and long legs – particularly the powerful hind legs that can help it attain speeds of 72km/h. When running the hare tucks its dark-topped white tail down, while the Rabbit does the opposite, so the fluffy white underside is visible as it hops along (*see centre photo, opposite page*).

The Brown Hare is not native to

Warrens

Rabbits are sociable animals, living in networks of burrows known as warrens. They particularly favour light and sandy soils that are easy to excavate.

Hierarchies exist within social groupings, each warren featuring dominant males and females. Females reach sexual maturity from just four months old and are able to give birth to a litter of 3–7 young roughly every month in spring and summer. The vast majority of kits do not make it past their first year, succumbing to illness or falling victim to predators.

While the lifespan of Rabbits in captivity may reach double figures, the average life expectancy in the wild is around 2–3 years.

and exposed soil created by their grazing and digging can benefit a variety of wildflowers and insects. They also play an important part in the food chain, being on the menu for a range of carnivores such as Foxes, Stoats and Buzzards.

Although they are usually quiet, Rabbits sound the alarm by thumping the ground and utter a scream when caught by a predator.

Rabbits are grey-brown in colour, but naturally occurring, entirely black variants may occasionally be spotted living in the wild.

Britain. It is believed to have arrived during or before Roman times. The current population is estimated at around 800,000.

The scarcer **Mountain Hare**, (*left*) which has shorter black-tipped ears than the Brown Hare, is native to Britain and is found on heather moorlands and uplands in Scotland and northern England. In winter its coat turns white, providing crucial camouflage in snowy conditions. A subspecies called the Irish Hare is found in Ireland.

Badger

Some mammals are so familiar that they hardly need introduction, the **Badger** among them. And yet, easy as it may be to identify such a widespread and one-of-a-kind species, these secretive, nocturnal animals tend to keep well out of sight.

A common view of a live Badger is the fleeting sighting of a low, heavy shape caught in car headlights as it crosses a country lane at night – white facial stripes shining in the beams like road markings. For such large and boldly marked mammals, Badgers have an impressive ability to evade us – making sightings of these unmistakable and charismatic animals all the more memorable.

If you encounter a Badger while on foot, perhaps foraging at dawn or dusk, it is that conspicuous black-and-white face which stands out above all else. These sturdy, short-legged mustelids, related to Stoats and Otters, have a pale tail and silvery-grey body. Occasional individuals have very light-coloured fur.

Badgers rely on a keen sense of smell, so may not detect people located downwind who remain quiet and still.

Their main food is earthworms, and they leave telltale scuff marks in lawns where they have been foraging. They can consume dozens of worms a night, and will also eat small mammals, Hedgehogs, berries and nuts. In the autumn they put on weight to help see them through the colder months when they are less active above ground.

Badgers usually mate in spring – though female implantation of the fertilised eggs is delayed until the following winter, with a litter of typically two or three cubs born early in the year. The playful

Communal living

Badgers are powerful diggers, with strong claws, and excavate burrows known as setts that have extensive tunnel systems as well as underground chambers for resting or raising young.

Often dug into a slope within the shelter of woodland, the setts have a number of entrances and, as expected given the size of the occupants, these holes are large and broad. Spoil heaps of excavated earth are piled up in front of the entrances and the

soil typically contains dried plant material used as bedding, which these tidy dwellers regularly replenish. Fox dens, on the other hand, lack multiple entrances and have a musky smell, while Rabbit holes are circular in shape and smaller.

Some well-established setts occupied by generations of Badgers are more than a century old.

Badgers are social and several adults and cubs may inhabit a sett. The evidence of activity is visible

young emerge from the sett in spring and are independent by late summer.

Badgers have been widely persecuted down the centuries. They are culled under licence in some areas under a controversial programme to prevent the spread of bovine tuberculosis. Large numbers are also killed on roads. Despite this, these protected mammals, with an average lifespan of 5–8 years, remain common across the country, inhabiting a range of habitats, and the greatest concentrations are found in the south-west.

Tracks and signs

Badgers follow regular routes around their home ranges, wearing well-trodden paths through vegetation. These can look like trails created by people, but they wind up and down banks, across lanes, and beneath hedgerows and fences.

Many woodland dwellers share pathways, though those created by deer won't pass low under a fence – and here you may find the straight grey, black or white hairs of a Badger caught in the twists of barbed wire.

The footprints, measuring roughly 4–5cm across, have large pads and forward-pointing toes tipped with the long marks of their non-retractable claws.

the vicinity, including scratch marks at the base of trees and shallow latrine pits scraped in the ground.

Organised Badger-watching sessions run at some active setts provide an opportunity to enjoy close encounters with individuals more accustomed to the proximity of people. Badgers are partial to unsalted peanuts, so a scattering of these can be used to encourage them to feed within view.

MAMMALS 17

Mole

No other mammal has quite such a visible presence and yet remains so impossibly difficult to see as the **Mole**. Molehills dotted across lawns and fields are a familiar sight – but very good luck is required to actually encounter a live Mole above ground.

These insectivores spend their lives underground, digging burrows which may lie just beneath the surface and up to a metre down. These tunnels provide a means to find food, as worms and other invertebrates fall into them.

The molehills, often in lines, are the piles of excavated earth, and larger mounds may lie above an underground nesting chamber.

Moles patrol their network of burrows for food and have short, velvety fur that can be brushed in any direction, easing movement forwards or backwards through narrow passageways. The fur can vary in colour, but is usually black or a dark earthy grey or taupe (the French word for Mole).

In the past, molecatchers sold their quarry's small pelts for use in the fashion industry, particularly during the early twentieth century. The fur sections were sewn together to trim hats, gloves and other garments for high society customers.

There are many species of mole worldwide, but only one in Britain – the European Mole, which is also widespread across the Continent. It can be found throughout Britain in suitable habitat – avoiding waterlogged areas – but is absent from Ireland.

Roughly 15cm long, Moles are thickset and have tiny eyes. However, they are not blind and can detect changes in light levels. They have a cylindrical body, small ear openings hidden

Molehills

Molehills map the excavations of these below-ground dwellers and the extent of individual territories. Deeper established tunnels, which may stretch over hundreds of metres, enable them to find food in freezing conditions or during times of drought, when worms may be driven deeper in the soil.

Other mammals create underground tunnels, and those of voles could be confused with Moles. However, vole tunnel

Raising young

Moles lead largely solitary lives in their tunnels below ground. Males detect females by sound and smell, and link burrows to find mates rather than risking popping above the surface.

Females raise a litter of three or four young in the spring in a nesting chamber which, along with resting chambers, typically lies beneath a larger molehill.

In late summer, the young leave their mother's tunnel territory and head off above ground to find their own patch of ground to call home. They do this at night under the cover of darkness in order to minimise the chances of falling victim to predators.

beneath their fur, a long snout, and powerful spade-like front feet equipped with strong claws for digging. High levels of oxygen-carrying haemoglobin in the blood enable them to cope with inferior air quality in their tunnels.

These active little mammals consume roughly half their body weight in food every day and worms make up the vast bulk of their diet. In times of plenty they may store fresh supplies of worms by biting the head section to immobilise them. They also eat other invertebrates such as insect larvae.

Largely safe underground, Moles can live between three to six years.

systems lie just beneath the surface, creating ridges in the ground, or run amid the roots of grasses. They are also smaller than the Mole's tunnels, and lack the telltale heaps of fresh earth.

The tunnelling of Moles helps aerate and drain heavy soils, but the soil spoil heaps they create are far from popular with gardeners, golf course managers and farmers. Unsightly molehills can be scraped of the surface with a spade, while various recommended methods to deter Moles may or may not be effective. They range from using certain plants or strong-smelling substances to repel them to placing vibrating toy windmills or ultrasonic devices above tunnels.

In wet weather Moles may be flooded out and emerge from their burrows, while the young also disperse above ground in summer. Moles may be killed by traffic when venturing across roads.

MAMMALS 19

Stoat

The **Stoat** is an energetic and elusive species that you tend to come across unexpectedly, perhaps dashing across a country path or searching out prey along a ditch, hedgerow or drystone wall.

While fairly common and widespread, this slender, short-legged predator is not especially easy to see. It stands low to the ground and sticks close to cover, moving rapidly and checking every nook and cranny as it hunts.

It is smart looking, with chestnut-brown upperparts neatly divided from its white underside, and has a long, black-tipped tail.

The Stoat feeds on small mammals, despatching catches with a bite to the back of the neck. It will also eat birds and eggs, and tackle prey much larger than itself – notably Rabbits.

Stoats are active throughout the year, by night and day, and live in diverse habitats where there is sufficient food, generally avoiding the depths of woodland.

Stoat or Weasel?

There is a well-worn humorous saying: '*A weasel is weasily recognised, while a stoat is stoatally different.*' But this doesn't really help when it comes to telling these lookalikes apart!

Both of these sinuous and feisty mustelids have gingery-brown fur and are light underneath. But the Stoat is the larger of the two – think of a Stoat as roughly the length of a cucumber and the Weasel as the length of a frankfurter sausage.

Given size is not always easy to assess in the field, the most reliable distinguishing feature is the telltale tail. In Stoats it is longer and tipped black, as if dipped in ink, while with Weasels it is shorter and lacks the dark tip. Stoats also have darker faces than Weasels, and the dividing line between their brown upperside and whitish underside is neater.

Unlike Stoats in northern areas of Britain, our Weasels don't have a white fur coat in winter.

Both Stoats and Weasels have been persecuted down the centuries. Stoats will kill poultry and gamebirds if they get into an enclosure, but smaller Weasels

In the colder months, Stoats living in northern Britain moult into a white coat to blend in better with snowy conditions – retaining the black end to the tail (*below*). The amount of white in the winter coat may vary and is absent in more southerly climes. A pure white Stoat is known as an Ermine, and the dense fur was historically used to make capes and collars embellishing the ceremonial robes of royals and peers – the pelts stitched together and spotted with the black tail tips.

While trapped in the past for its coat, the Stoat is also partial to using another's fur itself. It will take over the burrows of prey such as Rabbits and rats, and line the den with the warm fleece of its former resident.

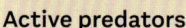

Active predators

Both Stoats and Weasels are ruthless and restless predators.

Stoats are large enough to tackle Rabbits and run with a bounding gait, pausing upright on their hind legs to view their surroundings or potential threats. Scampering slimline Weasels – the smallest of our carnivores – tend to hunt mice and voles, pursuing prey down their narrow burrows.

Weasels are wary and secretive hunters, mainly active at night, dawn or dusk, and are themselves preyed upon by Foxes, owls and Buzzards. The fortunes of Weasels are tied to the abundance of rodents. Each Weasel needs to eat a third of its body weight every day to survive.

Stoats breed between April and July, but implantation of the fertilised eggs is delayed so that, regardless of the time of mating, females give birth the following spring, raising large litters of 'kits'. During the breeding season males not only mate with adult females, but also with young females before they have left the nest.

While Stoats can survive for around five years, they more typically live between one and two years. The UK population is estimated at around 460,000 – much the same as that of the Stoat's smaller counterpart, the **Weasel**.

are unable to tackle large birds and instead act as useful pest controllers on farms by eating small rodents. In years when Field Voles are plentiful, female Weasels may raise two litters of 4–6 young, creating fur-lined nests in the empty burrows of their prey.

The Weasel has a short tail, which lacks the distinctive black tip that is a feature of the Stoat's tail.

MAMMALS 21

Otter

It is not surprising that the **Otter** remains something of a rare and special sighting, despite being a widespread and relatively large mammal.

For the most part it is nocturnal, and those that live alongside our rivers and lakes keep a low profile, hidden from view within the gullies carved by watercourses or screened by bankside vegetation.

When swimming, all that may be spotted is a head above the surface, carving a wake through the water, the long body largely submerged and thick, tapering tail helping steady it.

A chance encounter at dawn or dusk is likely to be brief, these wary mammals rapidly making off if they detect they are being watched. However, those Otters that hunt along the coast – particularly in Scotland – are often active in daylight, offering the chance of good views as they forage in the shallows and along the tideline (*right*).

It is a mistake to describe coastal populations as 'Sea Otters'. The Sea Otter is a different species altogether, found along the northern Pacific seaboard. In the British Isles, we have only one type of Otter, inhabiting both sheltered seashores and

Not quite an Otter?

The **American Mink** (*left*) is a river-dwelling mammal that could be confused with the Otter.

This non-native species escaped, and was deliberately released, from fur farms during the mid-twentieth century and has spread far and wide to become firmly established in the British Isles, outnumbering Otters and decimating populations of Water Voles upon which they prey, along with other rodents, fish and birds.

Mink are roughly half the size of an Otter and most are dark brown or black in colouring all over save for a tiny patch of white on the chin. A fleeting glimpse of a Mink crossing a canal or river in poor light might suggest an Otter.

The Mink is not such a strong or capable swimmer, paddling buoyantly and rapidly with much of its back above the surface, showing a shorter and fluffier tail than the Otter's long, thick-based

Tracks and signs

Otters mark their territories with their droppings, known as 'spraints'. These are deposited prominently, for example on the top of a rock, and when fresh they are dark and have a sweet or fishy smell – should you wish to test the bouquet!

Regularly used 'slides' where they enter the water are characterised by flattened vegetation and smoothed mud.

Other signs include half-eaten fish beside a river, and rounded footprints. Fresh prints in soft mud may sometimes show a faint web mark between the toes. More notable is a line scored in the mud where the Otter's tail has dragged on the ground.

inland waterways, wetland and lakeside habitats.

At one stage Otters were very scarce in Britain. A combination of persecution and river pollution – particularly agricultural chemicals in the food chain – saw numbers plummet by the 1970s. However, protection and improvement in water quality has seen them regain lost ground, so that today they number more than 10,000 and have been recorded in every river catchment system.

Otters live close to water where they hunt for fish – their main food – along with a variety of other prey. When foraging, these opportunistic carnivores may cover several kilometres along the coast and around estuaries, up rivers and through wetlands.

Males and females are generally solitary. Their dens, known as 'holts', may be tucked away within natural cover, rock crevices and bankside holes, or humanmade tunnels and old sea defences. They can breed at any time of year, though typically in the warmer months, and a female raises 2–3 cubs, which remain with her for roughly a year before moving on.

...ut tapering tail. The heftier ...tter is more at home in the water, ...wimming low and smooth. And in ...erms of body length, think dog for ...n Otter, and cat for a Mink.

The wild **Polecat** (*right*) is a ...milar size to a Mink and dark-...oated, though with a pale face ...at has a dark 'bandit mask' ...cross the eyes. Its heartland is ...ales, but it is steadily spreading ...d now numbers in the tens of ...ousands.

Red Deer

Majestic **Red Deer** stags crowned by impressive sets of antlers are among the most striking sights in nature. Particularly so when the bellowing males gather every year, often at traditional sites, to battle for supremacy and mating rights during the autumn 'rut'.

The largest native land mammal in the British Isles, the Red Deer stands more than a metre high at the shoulder. Despite their size, free-roaming individuals that inhabit woodlands can be surprisingly elusive, sometimes only venturing out into open areas to feed after dark or at dawn and dusk.

They are most common and easiest to view in Scotland, where they inhabit open moorland and hillsides on the mainland and islands. They are widespread and found in numbers on Exmoor, in the Quantocks, Cumbria, the New Forest, Peak District and East Anglia, among other areas, as well as in deer parks. Those living in southern woodlands tend to grow larger than individuals that inhabit harsher upland environments.

Stags and the slightly smaller and slimmer hinds (females) live apart in separate herds for most of the year, coming together for the rut, which takes place between late September and November. During this period dominant males gather a harem

Red Deer or Roe Deer?

Red Deer and Roe Deer are our most common deer species, with the population of Red Deer in Britain estimated at around 350,000 and Roe Deer numbering roughly 500,000.

They may be confused, given they both have a plain reddish-brown coat, which is also darker and greyer during winter. Both of these native species also lack black markings around the tail – the rear end being an important way of telling deer apart as they are often seen running away! The Roe Deer has a large whitish patch on its tufty rump, while the Red Deer has a short brown tail and pale cream rump (*right*).

Roe Deer have a black nose and white chin, and are smaller than Red Deer – as a simplistic guide to height, think goat for Roe Deer and cow for Red Deer.

Bucks – the name given to Roe Deer males – have very short, branched antlers compared with those of Red Deer stags. They bear no more than three points and are absent in does (Roe Deer females). The antlers are shed in early winter and regrow ahead of the rut, which takes place in late summer – earlier in the year than that of Red Deer.

Antlers

Red Deer stags grow antlers ahead of the annual rut. Mature individuals sport the largest and most formidable weaponry, bearing sometimes as many as 16 branching points.

The antlers are composed of bone and differ from the permanent horns of other hoofed mammals that are covered with keratin.

Red Deer antlers are shed ('cast') every spring, with new antlers regrowing beneath a layer of skin, which supplies blood-rich nutrients and is known as 'velvet' (*right*). Once the antlers are fully grown the velvet is sloughed off and the hard, bony headgear is complete.

Antlers are only found on male deer – **Reindeer** being the exception.

of females, which they defend against challengers.

Mated hinds give birth the following spring and summer, and the young, known as calves, have light spots on their coats for several months (*far left*). Adults are reddish-brown with a cream-coloured rump and very short brownish tail. The coat is darker and greyer in winter.

Of the six species of deer that live in Britain, Red Deer, along with **Roe Deer**, are the only truly indigenous species. The non-native **Sika Deer** (*see page 26*) has large antlers like those of the Red Deer.

Red Deer are closely related to American Elk and in the wild generally live between 10 and 16 years.

Browsing deer can damage crops and young trees. With no natural predators, numbers are culled to manage populations, as well as for sport and venison. They are also killed on our roads, with deer of all species in Britain involved in tens of thousands of vehicle collisions every year.

Both Roe Deer and Red Deer have a light patch on their rear. Roe Deer (*left*) lack an obvious tail and males have small antlers. The rump of Red Deer (*right*) is creamy, with a short brown tail.

MAMMALS

Fallow Deer

If asked to describe a deer, this is the species most likely to come to mind for many, with its distinctive flattened antlers, elegant features and white-spotted coat.

Fallow Deer are widespread and common, particularly across England – though like all our deer species they can be shy and elusive. They inhabit woods and fields, favouring deciduous woodland with open areas for grazing, and are often found in small herds.

Popular as stock for deer parks, Fallow Deer are more confident where they have become accustomed to humans. In such parks they may be easy to view and their attractive markings add to their appeal.

Unlike **Roe** and **Red Deer**, they are not native to Britain, but have become a long-established addition to our fauna. While there is evidence the Romans kept Fallow Deer in Britain, it was the Normans who introduced this species for good in the eleventh century. Fallow Deer were brought to our islands from the Mediterranean region for hunting and their meat, eventually escaping enclosures and estates and roaming free.

The antlers of males distinguish this medium-sized deer from other species, being flattened towards the top. The term 'palmate' – like the smooth palm of a hand – is used to describe this appearance. The Fallow Deer's spotted coat and notably black-and-white rear end also help separate the species from the smaller Roe Deer and larger Red Deer (*see page 24*).

Male Fallow Deer (referred to as 'bucks') shed their antlers in spring and grow a new set ahead of the autumn mating period known as the 'rut', when rivals compete for the attention of female

Not quite a Fallow Deer?

The non-native **Sika Deer** (*right*) is a similar size to the Fallow Deer, and in the summer it also has light spots on its flanks. However, Sika antlers are not flattened and the slender branching points resemble those of a Red Deer stag. The Sika Deer has a whitish rump, with a dark border – similar to the rear end of a Fallow Deer, but lacking the long black tail of the latter.

Sika Deer were introduced to Britain from East Asia in the 1860s

deer (which, as anyone who has watched *The Sound of Music* knows, are called 'does'!).

During the rut in October and November, mature bucks make guttural groaning noises, thrash the undergrowth with their antlers and battle for supremacy and breeding rights.

Along with eating grass and other vegetation, Fallow Deer are also partial to acorns, berries and beech mast. As with other deer, their browsing has an impact on forestry and crops. Straying onto roads, deer are frequently involved in traffic accidents.

Telltale tail

The Fallow Deer is reddish-brown and bears Bambi-like white spots on the back and sides. A light horizontal line is often visible along the flank close to the belly.

There is variation in colouring, with some individuals light and others very dark. In winter the coat is thicker and greyer, and the spotting less obvious.

The white rump patch is edged with black, while the longish, thin tail hanging down the middle is black on top. The effect looks a little as if the oval of white on the deer's rear has been painted with three vertical black lines.

and are related to Red Deer, with which they frequently interbreed to create hybrid offspring. Sika number more than 11,000 in Britain and are found in areas including the New Forest, Cumbria and northern and western Scotland.

The **Muntjac Deer** (*left*) is a very small, shy deer that hails from China. Now numbering tens of thousands in the wild, free-roaming Muntjac are mostly found in central, eastern and southern England. Stocky and hunched in build, they are no bigger than a medium-sized dog, and live in wooded habitats with dense undergrowth, including large suburban gardens. They have dark stripes running down the forehead, a white underside to the tail – revealed when fleeing – and make a repeated barking sound. The males have short little curved prongs for antlers.

MAMMALS 27

Brown Rat

Rats are not exactly our most popular mammals – which is something of an understatement. Yet these resourceful rodents are seldom far away, even if the saying that one is never more than a few metres from a rat is an urban myth.

We have two kinds of rat living in Britain – the widespread and abundant **Brown Rat** and the extremely rare **Black Rat**. Neither of them are native, hailing originally from Asia, but both became established several centuries ago and spread widely.

Rats carry diseases and can reach high densities if food resources allow – being associated with poor standards of hygiene.

The Brown Rat is greyish-brown and its tail is bare and rather thick. Rats and mice have similar features, but there is a large size disparity between these groups of rodents. The body of a typical mouse is approximately the length of a thumb, while a rat's body is roughly that of a hand – plus a tail almost as long again.

Brown Rats inhabit sewers, farm buildings and built-up areas and can be spotted beside canals, at rubbish tips and along the strandline of beaches. Opportunist omnivores, they may also become established in gardens where food is regularly provided for birds. Female Brown Rats may raise several litters of young per year.

Lookalike rodents

If you spot a rat in Britain it is almost certainly a Brown Rat. The **Black Rat** (*below centre*) is virtually extinct in this country. It was once our most abundant rat but has been driven out by the larger Brown Rat and targeted pest control, and is also less adapted to modern habitation and our damp climate.

The Black Rat is famously the species whose fleas carried the bubonic plague. Also known as the 'Ship Rat', these travellers and adept climbers may turn up at ports, but are difficult to tell apart from Brown Rats, given some

Black Rats have brown fur. Brown Rats are strong swimmers, which might lead to confusion with similar-sized **Water Voles**. The Water Vole (*below right*) lives along the well vegetated banks of rivers, dykes and marshes. Water Voles have smaller ears, a shorter tail and a snubbier nose than the rat. While widespread, the Water Vole has suffered a steep population decline.

House Mouse

We have a number of different mouse species in this country, and the best known is the **House Mouse**.

Widespread and abundant, the House Mouse is not that easy to spot, being wary and largely nocturnal. The species is found living in buildings – including houses, farm buildings, sheds, warehouses and garages – and is an opportunist, feeding on anything from grain to rubbish scraps.

It looks like a typical little mouse: grey-brown with a pointy face, small eyes and a long, thin tail.

Prodigious breeders, females can produce several litters of 5–8 young every year. As a result these unsanitary guests may reach pest proportions if conditions allow, and cause damage – for example by gnawing electric cabling.

Infestations are less common these days in domestic properties. If you have a mouse problem, they can be caught and released outside using humane traps, or you can seek advice from professional pest control services.

Cat owners are likely to come across small rodents when their pets proudly deposit catches, dead or alive, on the doorstep. A live mouse indoors tends to run around the edge of a room, seeking out cover, and may be caught by steering it into an empty cereal box placed flush against the skirting board.

Rural relatives

The common and widespread **Wood Mouse** (*below*) favours woodland, along with gardens, fields and verges – though can also be seen in buildings and sheds. Once known as the Long-tailed Field Mouse, it is warmer brown than the House Mouse and has prominent eyes and ears, and strong back legs that enable it to hop when escaping predators.

The Wood Mouse has a close lookalike called the **Yellow-necked Mouse**, which is uncommon and restricted to the southern half of Britain. It is more orangey-brown with, as the name suggests, a yellowish collar across its pale chest.

The final member of the mouse family in Britain is the tiny **Harvest Mouse** (*right*). It is light enough to live clambering among ground vegetation, using its prehensile tail to help secure a grip. It builds ball-shaped nests of woven grasses close to the ground.

Mice may be confused with blunter-nosed voles (*see page 30*) and long-snouted shrews (*see page 31*).

Bank Vole

Voles are similar in appearance to mice, but look chubbier with a less pointy face, smaller eyes and ears, and a shorter tail. A bit cuter, one might say.

There are three widespread British species of vole – the similar-looking **Bank Vole** and **Field Vole**, and the larger **Water Vole**.

The Bank Vole, the smallest of the bunch, can be found in all kinds of habitat, including gardens, grassland and scrub, but particularly favours wooded areas.

The Bank Vole has noticeably reddish-brown fur and is pale on its underside. These active little rodents live in shallow burrows, venturing from them to feed on leaves, insects, berries, fruit, nuts and seeds – which they may hoard underground to help see them through the winter as they don't hibernate.

As with many small mammals, the life expectancy of a Bank Vole is not long, given they are on the menu for a host of predators and also suffer in harsh winters. Two years is good going for an individual. Nevertheless, these voles are very common and widespread, numbering in the millions in the British Isles, with populations fluctuating from one year to the next depending on conditions and their breeding success.

Fellow voles

The Bank Vole has a lookalike – the **Field Vole** (*below right*), which is an abundant species that generally favours more open grassy habitats, as the name suggests.

Also known as the Short-tailed Vole, the Field Vole is preyed upon by a range of animals – including Kestrels, Barn Owls, Adders, Foxes and Stoats – so wisely endeavours to keep out of view beneath long grass, scampering along shallow tunnels and runways hidden within the tussocks. It is grey-brown, with small ears almost concealed by fur, while the Bank Vole is a richer chestnut-brown.

The declining Water Vole (*bottom, and page 28*) is the largest of our voles, being closer to the size of a rat, and lives beside water, into which it will dive with an audible 'plop'.

Voles are plump-looking and blunt-nosed, but may be confused with mice, which have larger eyes and ears (*see page 29*), and long-nosed shrews (*see page 31*).

Common Shrew

Shrews are pointier little mammals than mice and voles and have tiny eyes, small inconspicuous ears, velvety fur and a long, narrow nose for sniffing out food.

There are three main British species – the **Common Shrew**, the smaller **Pygmy Shrew** and the **Water Shrew**.

The Common Shrew is the commonest of the bunch – not that it is easy to spot. Its high-pitched twittering squeaks during territorial skirmishes might give its presence away in ground vegetation. You are perhaps more likely to come across one dead than alive, as some predators, like cats, find them unpalatable and discard their catch.

Shrews live life at a high pace, burning up energy at such a rate that they need to eat virtually their body weight every day in invertebrates, such as worms, spiders and beetles.

A large percentage of these hyperactive little insectivores do not make it through the winter and the production of large numbers of young in spring and summer is vital to keep population numbers healthy.

The Common Shrew is dark brown on top and pale beneath. It lives hidden by long grasses, ground vegetation, leaf litter and within burrows in habitats ranging from gardens and grasslands to woodland, hedgerows and road verges.

British shrews

The **Pygmy Shrew** (*below*) is very similar-looking to the Common Shrew but, as the name suggests, tiny – its head and body measuring a mere 4–6cm in length. Tail length can also help with identification. The Common Shrew's tail is proportionately only about half the length of its body, but the Pygmy Shrew's tail is well over half its body length, and is hairier.

The **Water Shrew** (*right*) is darker than the two other species, looking almost black above and white below. It lives near freshwater, feeding on invertebrates both on land and underwater – a fringe of hairs on its feet helps it paddle beneath the surface on short forays. Unusually for a mammal, it has venomous saliva, its bite enabling it to incapacitate prey larger than itself.

Much rarer are the **Lesser White-toothed Shrew**, found on the Isles of Scilly, and the **Greater White-toothed Shrew**, confined to the Channel Islands, parts of Ireland and north-east England.

Common Pipistrelle

The **Common Pipistrelle** is our most numerous and widespread species of bat. It can commonly be seen fluttering around gardens and along woodland edges, or circling street lights – jinking and turning suddenly as it snatches flying insects.

Its brown furry body is smaller and lighter than that of a House Mouse, weighing about the same as a 20p coin, while each wing is roughly the size of a credit card.

Because of its size, it tends to feed on small prey and can consume up to 3,000 midges, mosquitos and other little insects at night. Pipistrelles often follow habitual flight paths when feeding, such as repeatedly passing alongside a house wall on a circuit.

In the summer, young are raised in 'maternity roosts', which can contain dozens of females. Such

Observing bats

We have 18 species of bat in Britain. But they are challenging to observe and tell apart, especially as they are mainly active after dark and hide away by day. In addition, all of our species, and their breeding sites and resting places, have legal protection against disturbance.

The best way to learn about our bats, enjoy closer encounters or be sure of what you are spotting is to join an organised evening bat walk, typically led by a licensed expert.

Identifying bats in flight generally means using a bat detector – a handheld device that can be tuned into the bursts of high-frequency sound bats use to navigate and find prey. Bats are not blind, but at night they see with their ears! They emit high-pitched shrieks and listen with their sensitive ears for the echoes bouncing off obstacles, mapping their surroundings from the strength and direction of

Hibernation

All British bats eat insects, taking advantage of the smorgasbord of moths, beetles and mosquitos on the wing after dark during the warmer months.

But an appetite for airborne food comes at a price: flying burns up a huge amount of energy. In the winter, when there are few insects active and keeping warm is a trial, bats hibernate, allowing their metabolic levels to fall as they slip into a torpor. Tucked away in caves, tunnels, cellars and crevices, they are sustained in this state of inactivity by their fat reserves.

Females raise young in summer maternity roosts, typically located in tree holes, buildings or bat boxes, while males seek shelter elsewhere.

roosts may be located in a tree hole, a suitable bat box or behind hanging house tiles and roof boards. The young – known as 'pups' (*left*) – are independent about six weeks after being born.

Bats that inhabit lofts or wall cavities may be heard as they utter audible squeaking social calls. Their presence can be confirmed by droppings, which are typically the size of rice grains, dark and crumbly, containing tiny insect parts.

During the cold winter months, pipistrelles hibernate in nooks and crannies, in small groups or individually.

The Common Pipistrelle has a close relative that is virtually identical in appearance and was only distinguished as a separate species in the 1990s: the **Soprano Pipistrelle**. As the name suggests, this lookalike makes a higher-pitched echolocation call, which can be recognised using a bat detector (*see below left*).

Bats are mysterious and fascinating, and the more you learn about these harmless insect-eaters, the more you begin to appreciate their adaptations to a nocturnal lifestyle, the challenges they face to survive, and their unique characteristics.

You also gain an appreciation of their vulnerability, given how precarious populations are. Out of sight beyond the closed curtains of our windows at night, these small, social mammals have suffered steep declines and some British bats rank among the rarest of our native fauna.

these reflected sounds.

A bat detector converts their ultrasonic echolocation calls, far beyond our hearing, into audible sounds. The range of frequencies and nature of these squeaks and warbles, which have an otherworldly quality, enable species to be recognised.

Bats can also be surveyed by counting them as they emerge from known roosts in tree holes, bat boxes or built structures like barns (*right*).

Brown Long-eared Bat

The **Brown Long-eared Bat** lives up to its name, having extremely long ears – nearly the length of its body. These large ears are sensitive enough to hear moths flying and detect the rustling sounds of insects that can be plucked off tree foliage.

At rest in roosts the Brown Long-eared Bat tucks its unwieldy ears under its wings or curls them up so that they resemble a ram's horns.

This widespread and relatively numerous species is most at home in woodland habitats, including parks and gardens. It typically flies close to trees in order to locate prey, such as moths and beetles. Catching insects on the wing is known as 'hawking' while snatching them from leaves is referred to as 'gleaning', and Brown Long-eared Bats are specialists in the latter technique, their broad wings helping them to manoeuvre.

They tend to fly relatively slowly compared with high-energy pipistrelles, and their long ears may even be visible as they flutter past.

Bat boxes

Much like birds, bats will take up residence in specially designed boxes – which can provide vital shelter in places with limited natural roosting sites.

A variety of types of box can be bought and they should be fixed high up on buildings and trees, preferably sheltered from prevailing winds and away from light sources. A clear flight path to the box, without obstacles such as branches in the way, enables bats to come and go unimpeded.

Bat boxes have vertical landing boards and narrow entrances, which prevent birds moving in. Wooden boxes – which are relatively simple to make – should be left untreated, as chemicals can be toxic to bats.

Installing several boxes facing

Brown Long-eared Bats make very quiet echolocation noises when hunting so they can listen out for insects. This stealthy approach makes these so-called 'whispering bats' challenging to pick up using a bat detector.

During the warmer months, Brown Long-eared Bats roost in buildings, including loft spaces, churches and barns, as well as in suitable bat boxes. In general, they tend to stick close to their sheltered roosting sites when out foraging, typically emerging to feed up to an hour after sunset.

Bats congregate to breed in the autumn, although delayed ovulation means the females don't give birth until the following summer. They raise their young, known as 'pups', in group maternity roosts'.

In the winter, Brown Long-eared Bats seek out quiet, safe places to hibernate that have a stable, cold temperature, such as cellars, caves, mines and tunnels.

For their size, bats are remarkably long-lived, and Brown Long-eared Bats can live for up to 30 years.

The Brown Long-eared Bat has a virtually identical relative called the **Grey Long-eared Bat** – an extremely rare species mainly found in southern and western England. The two long-eared lookalikes require expert knowledge to tell apart.

Varied species

We have 18 regularly occurring species of bat in Britain. Accurate identification may require a bat detector (*see page 32*) or close-up observations by a licensed expert.

Among the variety of species are **Greater** and **Lesser Horseshoe** bats – named after their distinctive horseshoe-shaped nose. They are found in southern and westerly Britain, and at rest hang upside down with their wings wrapped around their body (*below*).

The **Serotine** is a large species which typically roosts in older buildings and is mainly found in southern England.

British scarcities include the **Bechstein's Bat**, the **Barbastelle** and the extremely rare **Greater Mouse-eared Bat**, which has declined to just one or two individuals.

in different directions gives bats more options. They are fussy tenants so patience is required – it may take years before any take up residence, if at all.

Given bats are protected by law from disturbance, the best way to know if a box is occupied is to watch at sunset for any comings and goings. You can also listen out for 'chattering' noises inside the box or check below the entrance for any small, crumbly black droppings that have fallen out.

Noctule

Many of our bats are difficult to identify without specialist echolocation detection equipment and expert know-how. However, the **Noctule** is a species that can be identified by sight, even by those without much experience of these secretive nocturnal mammals.

Our largest breeding bat, the Noctule typically emerges early in the evening before it gets dark. As the sun is setting, this Starling-sized species heads off to feed, flying fast and high. Above the treetops or over fields, it travels straight and direct, suddenly swooping down to snatch an insect before resuming its level flight path. Very different to the low, rapid twisting of little pipistrelles or the unhurried flappy flight of long-eared bats.

The Noctule has a robust body, with ginger-brown fur, and its narrow, pointed wings are built for speed. Close up it has a rather fearsome-looking demeanour, with short, rounded ears, a dark muzzle and pointed teeth.

This widespread woodland species hides away by day in tree holes, bat boxes and occasionally buildings. In late summer and early autumn, males attract females to mating roosts with shrill calls and successful individuals may gather a small harem. Delayed ovulation means the young are born the following summer and raised in female-only maternity roosts.

Bat facts

Bats resemble flying mice, and the German for bat is exactly that: *fledermaus*. However, despite similarities in appearance, bats are not even closely related to rodents.

Worldwide there are more than 1,400 species of bat – ranging from the tiny Bumblebee Bat with a body length less than 4cm to the Giant Golden-crowned Flying Fox, which has a 1.7-metre wingspan.

Bats are the only kinds of mammal that truly fly – as opposed to gliding. They have elongated finger bones over which the thin membrane of their wings is spread.

The leg and hip joints of bats bend in ways that enable them to hang from vertical surfaces, gripping with tiny claws, but they are ungainly on the ground, crawling clumsily.

All British bats depend upon insects for food and raise young when prey is plentiful during the warmer months. In winter they are forced to hibernate – however, they occasionally wake to feed when conditions allow.

Daubenton's Bat

If you find yourself beside a lake, canal or river on a summer's evening, you may spot **Daubenton's Bats** fluttering low over the water. Circling and turning in the fading light, they reveal a pale belly, contrasting with darker upperparts.

Sometimes referred to as 'water bats', they typically hunt flying insects just above still or slow-moving water, occasionally skimming the surface to catch prey. It is this feeding technique, coupled with a silvery-grey underside, which helps distinguish this widespread and relatively common bat from other species.

The Daubenton's Bat – named after an eighteenth-century French naturalist – flies with rapid wingbeats, sweeping back and forth as it targets midges, caddisflies, mayflies and other water-loving insects. It snatches them with its jaws or sometimes scoops them up using its tail membrane and bristly feet.

In the summer these bats, which are a little bigger than pipistrelles, tend to roost close to water, under bridges or in tree holes, while during winter they hibernate in tunnels or caves.

The Daubenton's Bat may be confused with the **Natterer's Bat**, which is a similar size and also has light fur on its underparts. Natterer's Bats frequently hunt over water, though tend to fly higher, rather than skimming just above the surface.

Threats to bats

Unlike other small mammals, bats don't build nests in which to raise young or keep warm in winter. Instead, they rely on 'roost' sites and may occupy several sheltered places during the year. The loss of these sites, due to the felling of mature trees, demolition of old buildings or conversion of lofts and barns, puts colonies at risk. All of our bat species and their roosts have legal protection.

Widespread declines in invertebrate numbers – caused by such factors as pesticide use and habitat loss – deprive bats of the insect food they require.

Our warming climate and more extreme weather patterns also impact their ability to feed and hibernate. Bats depend upon consistent cold conditions during winter to remain in a deep torpor – waking during mild spells burns up precious fat reserves.

Additional threats include collisions with road traffic, attacks by cats and light pollution.

Seals

You might imagine that a large mammal such as a seal would be pretty easy to identify. But when they are bobbing about close to shore, with just the head showing, or hauled out and dozing motionless amid tangles of seaweed, they are easy to overlook. All of a sudden that 'grey buoy' turns and submerges, or an individual among the sleeping sprawl on the rocks twitches its tail, and you wonder how you could ever have failed to spot them.

But what species of seal are you looking at? Two different species live around the coastline of the British Isles: the **Common Seal** and the **Grey Seal**. Despite their names, the latter is the more common of the two.

The Common Seal is mainly found in our northern waters and along the east coast, while the larger Grey Seal is more widespread, favouring exposed rocky shores, such as along the south-west coast. Scotland boasts large numbers of both species.

Their sleek covering of fur varies in colouring, darkness and markings, so is not a particularly reliable way of telling the species apart – though

Grey Seal

Although Grey Seals are common around the British Isles, they are rare globally.

They are the larger of our two seal species. Their coat is often grey in colouring as the name suggests, but can also be light or dark brown and mottled – a real blotchy hotch-potch. When hauled out they reveal a lighter underside, which differs from the more uniform back and belly of the Common Seal.

The long muzzle that helps distinguish this species from the Common Seal is more pronounced in males, which typically have a darker coat than females and young.

Common Seal

The Common (or Harbour) Seal is a gregarious species, congregating in numbers at favoured 'haul-outs' – typically sheltered bays, estuaries and sand flats.

Out of water these seals sometimes hold their body in a curved 'banana' posture, with head and tail slightly raised.

Common Seals may be grey, brown or blonde, with variable colouring and speckled markings. They have a compact muzzle and appealing eyes.

They give birth in summer. Pups can swim a few hours after being born and are a similar colour to adults. This differs from Grey Seal pups which are born later in the year and are creamy white for the first few weeks.

Among mottled adults the Grey Seal is typically more blotchy, while the Common Seal is more uniformly speckled.

Instead it is their faces that hold the key to distinguishing the species – which is just as well as this may be all that is visible when these inquisitive marine mammals are in the water. The Grey Seal has a long muzzle giving it something of a 'Roman' nose (*below left*), while the Common Seal has a snubby muzzle and more noticeable forehead (*below right*) – think horse-like face, versus puppy-like face.

The nostril slits of the Grey Seal are almost parallel, differing from those of the Common Seal which are 'V' shaped and nearly meet at the bottom.

Seals belong to a taxonomic grouping known as the pinnipeds, which translates 'fin footed'. Common and Grey seals are opportunist and generalist hunters, eating fish, squid, shellfish and sometimes seabirds.

Both of our resident species have legal protection and when hauled out to rest they should be viewed at a distance to avoid disturbance – particularly at breeding colonies.

Grey Seals often haul out on beaches, sandbars, rocky shorelines and islands, especially after long foraging trips or during the breeding season. When hunting for food they can travel tens of kilometres from land, diving to depths of over 300m.

Grey Seals give birth in secluded bays, not in the spring like much of our wildlife but in autumn and winter. The single white-furred pup is born out of water and remains on the beach, where it is fed on its mother's rich milk, rapidly gaining weight before it is able to fend for itself. Females tend to be the longer-lived of the sexes, reaching 30-plus years.

Dolphins

Few marine animals are as enthralling to watch as dolphins. Witnessing these charismatic cetaceans leaping close to shore or riding the bow wave of a boat is a mesmerising and memorable experience.

Powerful swimmers, supremely adapted to their aquatic environment, these social and intelligent marine mammals act as important indicators of the health of our seas, positioned as they are at the top of the food chain.

Dolphins also have a playful nature and appear to engage in acrobatic displays just for the fun of it, certainly bringing joy to those who encounter them at close quarters.

Fortunately, dolphins are a relatively common sight around our coastline. The difficulty can come

Bottlenose Dolphin

This large, playful and intelligent marine mammal is the most frequently observed dolphin around the British Isles, with some resident groups – or 'pods' – providing reliable sightings for dolphin-watching boat trips.

Acrobatic and smart, the species is perhaps most familiar as the type of dolphin kept in marine parks for public displays, and used in research on animal intelligence.

The Bottlenose Dolphin is robust and fairly plain grey, fading

with identifying cetaceans – the group that also includes whales and porpoises. We may only get fleeting glimpses as they surface – a head, blowhole, dorsal fin and tail – before they disappear into the depths once again.

From the fragments of the whole we have to piece together clues to work out what we are looking at. And it isn't made any easier by the fact that they are mobile, can stay submerged for an impressive length of time between breaths, and it's very difficult to predict exactly where they may pop up again for a lungful of air.

Of the various dolphins found around the British coast, the two most frequently sighted are the **Bottlenose Dolphin** and the **Common Dolphin**. In addition, our inshore waters play host to the smaller **Harbour Porpoise** (see page 42), which is also a resident breeding species and present year-round.

The highly social Bottlenose Dolphin is the largest of the three and the most easily seen. Bottlenose Dolphins have a short, stubby snout – or 'beak' – and a large sickle-shaped dorsal fin. They are plain grey – darker above and lighter below, while the slender Common Dolphin has cream and white on its sides. The shy Harbour Porpoise is dark-backed and has a small triangular dorsal fin.

Common Dolphin

This offshore species can frequently be spotted feeding close to land, and large, fast-moving pods make for a spectacular sight as they cut through the surface and leap above the water.

The Common Dolphin (also known as the Short-beaked Dolphin) has a dark back contrasting with a pale horizontal hourglass pattern of cream and white on the sides – differing from the plainer grey appearance of the heftier Bottlenose Dolphin.

The Common Dolphin's sleek body, long snout, slightly curved-back triangular dorsal fin and eye-catching markings make this an attractive species. Though it is harder to spot from land than the Bottlenose, it will sometimes swim alongside boats at impressive speeds.

Although protected, our dolphins are vulnerable to disturbance and threatened by overfishing; plastic, chemical and noise pollution; boat collisions and entanglement in hazardous fishing gear.

a paler shade on the flanks and belly, though some are darker in appearance. It also has a fairly stubby 'beak' – thick like a wine bottle, rather than the more pointed snout of a Common Dolphin. The Bottlenose Dolphin's dorsal fin is tall and curved backwards, so that it looks almost hooked.

Bottlenose Dolphins are sociable, typically found in groups rather than singly. A resident population of several hundred around Britain remain in localised inshore areas year-round, while more mobile offshore pods visit our waters.

Individuals can be recognised by the marks of healed scars on their dorsal fin. Photographic records help with identifying individuals and tracking movements.

Reliable places to see Bottlenose Dolphins, from land or on a dedicated dolphin-watching boat trip, include the Moray Firth in Scotland, Cardigan Bay in Wales, and around the coast of Cornwall. They are less common off eastern England.

Harbour Porpoise

The **Harbour Porpoise** is the smallest of all the cetaceans in British waters. It is also the most numerous inshore species.

However, you wouldn't necessarily know it, as Harbour Porpoises don't draw attention to themselves like more showy dolphins that ride boat bow waves, leap and frolic. Instead, shy porpoises keep a low profile, discreetly breaking the surface with a rolling motion.

They have blunt snouts rather than long beaks like dolphins – not that you can spot this easily as Harbour Porpoises typically remain low in the water when coming up for a swift intake of air. The best way to identify them is by their small size and the short triangular fin on their dark back – very different from the large, curved dorsal fin of dolphins.

Harbour Porpoises tend to be found in small groups or even as solitary individuals, commonly in coastal bays, estuaries and around headlands. They often hunt close to the seabed and are vulnerable to entanglement in fishing nets.

Two Harbour Porpoises swimming side by side may be a female accompanied by her offspring, or 'calf'.

The word porpoise derives from the Latin for pig, and these stocky cetaceans are colloquially known as 'puffing pigs' because of the sound they make when exhaling as they surface to breathe.

Variety of species

Globally there are eight species of porpoise. While they superficially resemble dolphins, porpoises are smaller and have teeth that are flatter in shape, among other differences, and are more closely related to the Beluga and Narwhal.

Some 28 species of dolphin, whale and porpoise have been recorded in UK waters, so there is always the possibility of spotting something out of the ordinary – especially on marine wildlife-watching boat trips.

Risso's Dolphin (*below*) is regularly recorded around Britain, most frequently off western coasts in late summer. It has a blunt, 'beakless' head, a high, curved dorsal fin, and its skin becomes scarred and noticeably whiter with age.

The **White-beaked Dolphin**, also less common and mainly seen around Scotland and in the North Sea, has a short, white-tipped beak and pale grey patches on its flanks, as well as a distinctive light 'saddle' on the back behind the dorsal fin.

Minke Whale

This is the whale most often encountered off the coast of the British Isles, especially as it will feed in shallow water relatively close to land and is also inquisitive enough to pay boats a visit.

Minke Whales (pronounced 'minky') may be spotted on marine wildlife-watching trips, from ferries or even from headlands on calm days, particularly in summer and autumn.

While not one of the huge leviathans of the oceans, the Minke Whale is awe-inspiring nonetheless at 7–9m long and several tonnes in weight.

Its distinguishing feature when coming up to breathe is its relatively small, hooked dorsal fin set far to the rear of its dark back (*inset*). Minke Whales also have white markings like 'armbands' across the front flippers.

Minke Whales are the smallest of the filter-feeding baleen whale family. They lunge into shoals of small fish and krill, gulping mouthfuls and sieving them from the seawater using brush-like plates which hang from the upper jaw.

Minke Whales only rarely breach – that is, leap out of the water. Instead they are fairly inconspicuous, surfacing quickly to breathe with a smooth rolling motion.

Good places to spot them include inshore waters around the western isles of Scotland, Cornwall and north-east England.

Whales in our waters

A number of whale species can be found around the British Isles – although spotting them is largely a matter of luck. However, you can improve the odds of an encounter by joining marine wildlife-watching trips.

The **Humpback Whale** (*near right*) is dark on top and has a small, stubby dorsal fin situated towards the rear end of its back. It has a rather flat head and very large white flippers. When diving it reveals its broad tail, which has black-and-white markings on the underside. This species can be showy at times, breaching and slapping the water with flippers and tail.

Other possible sightings include the vast and slender **Fin Whale**; the **Long-finned Pilot Whale**, which has a bulbous head and thick, swept-back dorsal fin; and the **Orca**, or Killer Whale, which is regularly spotted around the Shetland Isles and has distinctive black-and-white markings and a tall dorsal fin (*below*).

MAMMALS

Reptiles and amphibians

Common Frog

From Beatrix Potter's Jeremy Fisher to Kermit the Muppet, the frog has always been considered a likeable and eccentric character, big-eyed and full of bounce.

While a familiar species, the **Common Frog** may be confused with the **Common Toad** (*see page 48*) as they share many similarities.

The Common Frog is long legged and smooth skinned, with just the odd little lump and bump. It has a slight ridge on either side of the back, dark bands across the legs and a dark patch behind each eye. Generally olive-brown or greenish-grey, the colour and markings can vary, with some reddish or yellow in hue and individuals may be light or dark.

Adults spend much of the year feeding away from water, catching insects, slugs, snails and worms with their long sticky tongue, and spend the winter hidden in a crevice or even submerged at the muddy bottom of a pond.

During the breeding season, males develop dark swellings on their 'thumbs', called nuptial pads, which enable them to clasp firmly onto females as rivals tussle for mating rights.

Clumps of spawn laid in early spring contain up to 2,000 eggs, and breeding frogs can be heard croaking – particularly at night – as they congregate in shallow water, such as ponds, ditches and the margins of lakes. Unlike toads they are not faithful to their birthplace and are opportunistic when it comes to breeding sites, though often return to the pond from which they originated.

The froglets that develop from tadpoles leave the pond between July and September, and take two to three years to reach breeding age.

Frogspawn

Witnessing the wonder of metamorphosis as frogspawn eggs become tadpoles and grow into springy little froglets is fascinating for all ages.

The Common Frog lays spawn containing thousands of eggs in gelatinous clumps in shallow water and even temporary pools, which may dry out before the young have left. Toads wrap strings of eggs around vegetation, while newts lay single eggs on the leaves of pond plants.

46 REPTILES AND AMPHIBIANS

Rearing tadpoles

Small quantities of frogspawn can be reared in an aquarium or container, before returning the young to the same pond they were collected from to avoid unwittingly spreading disease.

Rainwater or pond water is better than tap water, which contains potentially harmful chemicals and should be left to stand for a day or two.

Tadpoles should be supplied with greens such as lettuce or boiled spinach leaves. As they grow they require protein-rich food and can be fed shop-bought fish flakes for coldwater fish.

As their legs develop, the growing froglets need to be able to climb out of the water onto stones to breathe air, or they can drown.

Ponds without fish tend to have healthier amphibian populations, as fish eat tadpoles – as will other animals, including dragonfly larvae.

Frogs tend to breed earlier than toads in the UK, with activity peaking from late February to March. The south-west usually records the first frogspawn sightings of the year. Really early spawn at the surface runs the risk of being killed if the temperature falls and the water freezes.

In adulthood frogs are vulnerable to predation, being on the menu of herons and Hedgehogs, Stoats and Grass Snakes, Foxes, Otters, rats and owls.

Resembling jelly-encased full stops, the dark embryos of frogspawn gradually take on the shape of commas before the punctuation marks swim free as tadpoles. Back legs eventually develop, followed by front legs, while the tail is absorbed into the body and lungs form, enabling the growing froglets to exit the water and breathe fresh air.

Newly hatched tadpoles feed on algae growing on pond plants and rocks exposed to sunlight. They begin life as herbivores but become omnivorous as they get older, feeding on decaying matter and tiny animals such as insects and their larvae.

It is believed that only around 1 in 50 frogspawn eggs actually makes it out of the water after three to four months as a fully formed froglet – so having dense rafts of spawn in a pond doesn't mean that your garden will be overrun with little frogs come the summer.

Common Toad

The **Common Toad** is found in a range of habitats across Britain and, in keeping with our other amphibians, returns to ponds and lakes to breed in the spring.

It is a species with mixed cultural associations, ranging from the wealthy and vain comic character Mr Toad of Toad Hall in *Wind in the Willows* to more sinister connections with witchcraft down the ages and the myth that touching one would give you warts.

Toads do have 'warty' skin, covered in bumps – which helps distinguish them from frogs – and the skin contains toxins distasteful to predators.

Usually brown or olive-brown in colour, toads can be quite dry to the touch when found out of water and are less dependent than other common amphibians on damp habitats.

Amphibians

Britain has seven native species of amphibian – three widespread kinds of newt (Palmate, Smooth and Great Crested) along with the Common Toad, Natterjack Toad, Common Frog and the rare, reintroduced Pool Frog.

These characterful and often endearing-looking animals make for fascinating viewing. Rearing tadpoles is one of the ways children may first connect with nature, and amphibians provide excellent pest-eating companions for gardeners.

All of our amphibians are aquatic for at least part of their life cycle, with adults returning to water to breed. As the skin of amphibians is not waterproof, like that of reptiles, they risk desiccation and predominantly live in damp habitats when on land.

In global terms amphibians are successful animals, with thousands of species and origins stretching back to the swamps of the Carboniferous period some 35 million years ago. They tend to be

Their back legs don't have the dark bands found on the **Common Frog** (*see page 46*) and are shorter, as they generally walk rather than hop. Toads also lack the thin ridge present on either side of a frog's back, though do have glandular swellings, a bit like ears, just behind each eye.

Common Toads are most easily spotted in spring when they return to their breeding ponds, often in numbers. During this period they are especially vulnerable when migrating across roads to reach favoured locations.

While the Common Frog is content to breed in shallow pools and is less faithful to ancestral sites, the Common Toad prefers deeper water bodies, including well established ponds, lakes and reservoirs.

Unlike frogs, toads don't lay their spawn in clumps, but instead in strings wrapped around pond vegetation (*below*). The dark toad tadpoles have skin toxins, just like adults, which make them unpalatable to predators such as fish. They emerge from ponds as toadlets in the summer,

Natterjack Toad

Britain is home to two kinds of toad: the Common Toad and the far rarer **Natterjack Toad**.

The Natterjack Toad is a native species confined to a few scattered heaths, coastal marshes and dunes, where it breeds at night in shallow pools. It can be distinguished from the Common Toad by its shorter legs and the pale yellow stripe running down the centre of its back. Males repetitively croak after dark beside breeding pools in spring, making a particularly loud rasping call.

This protected species has been the focus of concerted conservation efforts. Natterjack Toads can best be seen on guided walks at known breeding sites.

approximately four months after being laid as spawn.

Adult toads can live for around 10–12 years in the wild and eat a range of foods, including slugs, ants, beetles and other invertebrates. They are most active at night, hiding by day in a favoured sheltered hollow. During the winter they tuck themselves away in a burrow or beneath a compost heap, log pile or leaf litter.

found in warmer areas of the world is, while not strictly 'cold blooded', they rely on external heat to keep active.

Amphibians are, however, the most threatened group of vertebrates in the world. Habitat loss, climate change and disease are taking their toll on many species. A lethal infectious fungal disease, chytridiomycosis or 'chytrid', has spread rapidly around the globe, and has been present in the UK since 2004.

Fossil remains show amphibians have origins stretching back hundreds of millions of years.

Smooth Newt

We have three native species of newt in Britain. Two of them (the **Smooth Newt** and **Palmate Newt**) are common and quite similar-looking, while the third and largest (the **Great Crested Newt**) is far more distinctive but much scarcer.

Out of water, newts may be mistaken for lizards, though are much slower moving and lack the scaly skin of reptiles. You could say there is a hard and fast rule for telling them apart: scaly reptilian lizards are just that – hard to touch and fast when active. Velvety skinned newts are soft and slow.

Outside the breeding season, when newts feed and roam in damp places away from water, they tend to be fairly unexceptional in appearance. However, in spring and early summer when they return to ponds to breed, male newts of all our species are more impressive-looking and easier to identify.

Adult male Smooth Newts (*above*) are particularly handsome in the breeding season, sporting dark spots on their sides and a wavy crest that runs all the way down the body and tail (the jagged crest of the Great Crested Newt only runs down the back of its body).

Female Smooth Newts lack a crest and are more uniform brown, though often patterned with small dark spots, including on the throat (differing from the plain, pale throat of the similar Palmate Newt).

Male newts display to females in the water, fanning pheromones towards them. The females don't deposit clumps of spawn like frogs, or strings like toads, but instead lay individual eggs on the leaves of water vegetation. These develop into tiny newt tadpoles, known as larvae, that have frilly external gills. Eventually they develop legs and the juveniles typically leave the water in late summer,

Palmate Newt

The Palmate Newt gets its name from the webbed back feet of breeding males – the joined black toes spread like the palm of a hand. This feature is a useful way to identify them as they are quite similar to the Smooth Newt, though far less fancy-looking in the breeding season.

Palmate Newts, roughly a finger-length in size, are our smallest newt. The males are dark olive or brown with dark spots on the sides. As well as the black webbed back feet, the tip of the male's tail has a little filament sticking out of the end, like a stripped fuse wire. Females are lighter in colour and quite plain. When found away from water,

Great Crested Newt

The Great Crested Newt is by far the largest of our three species, growing to around 15cm in length.

These newts have a rough and warty skin, are blackish-brown with white speckling on their sides, and have an orange, spotted belly. Breeding males have an impressive jagged crest running the length of their body, earning them the nickname of 'dragons'.

This protected species, which has suffered declines due to habitat loss, is widespread, though less common in western areas of Britain. It generally breeds in large ponds, small lakes or flooded mineral workings – the males engaging in elaborate tail fanning courtship displays – and is most easily spotted at night during the spring breeding season by searching water margins with a torch after dark.

The Great Crested Newt is relatively long-lived and can reach 14-plus years in the wild.

reaching sexual maturity at between two and four years of age.

The Smooth Newt, sometimes known as the Common Newt, is found throughout Britain, with the largest concentrations in the south and east, and frequently inhabits garden ponds.

Newts tend to breed a little later in spring than frogs and toads, and may be present in ponds at various life stages throughout the year.

A female Smooth Newt, which lacks the jagged crest present on breeding males.

both sexes can appear gingery-brown.

They are best observed by torchlight at night, and if you manage to pick one up and carefully flip it onto its back, you will see it has a plain throat, differing from the dark spotting on that of the Smooth Newt.

Palmate Newts like shallow pools and favour slightly acidic water found in ponds on heathland and moorland. The species is more abundant in the west of Britain, while the Smooth Newt is the more common of the two in the east.

Newts lay their eggs individually on aquatic vegetation rather than depositing clumps or strings of spawn.

Garden ponds

If you want to boost biodiversity in your garden, just add water.

Digging a pond, however small, rewards all the effort at surprising speed. In fact, some wildlife, including dragonflies, may move in before you have even have a chance to put away the spade and hose and admire your handiwork.

The simple act of creating a watery wildlife sanctuary is virtually guaranteed to attract everything from amphibians to invertebrates. And the loss of ponds across the wider countryside, as land has been drained for agriculture and development, means gardens have become increasingly important refuges for freshwater species.

A typical garden pond can harbour a wealth of life both above and below the surface. It is likely to attract dragonflies, such as the **Broad-bodied Chaser**, delicate damselflies, including the **Large Red Damselfly**, and beetles like busy little **Common Whirligigs** and impressive **Great Diving Beetles**. Other invertebrates taking up residence include pond snails, **Pond Skaters** and **Water Boatmen**, while the aquatic refuge will act as a magnet for frogs and newts. Ponds also offer a source of drinking water for mammals such as **Hedgehogs**, and the insect life they support provides food for birds and bats.

and ensure it is safe regarding potential risks with small children.

When digging and lining a pond, it is worth choosing a site that is warm, sunny and sheltered, though not directly underneath a tree, which can clog the water with fallen leaves. Shallow areas as well as deep are important, avoiding steep sides all the way around that could prevent some species crawling in and out.

Sharp stones should be removed from the freshly dug hole and a layer of sand or old carpet placed over the surfaces to help ensure nothing will puncture the waterproof liner. Around the edges the liner can be trimmed once the pond is filled and hidden from view with turf or flagstones.

It is preferable to use rainwater, but a pond can be filled with tap water. The chlorine in standing tap water takes a few days to dissipate, or you can use a pond water treatment product.

Creating a pond

Garden ponds can be whatever size suits one's ambitions, budget and the space available. A tub, half-barrel or wheelbarrow basin may be transformed into a small water feature. Alternatively, you can buy a ready-made pond mould or excavate and line a larger area to create a pool. Materials and aquatic plants are readily available from garden centres and there are plenty of guides with expert advice on how to create a pond

▶ When creating a pond ensure it has a variety of depths. Shallow sides enable animals to climb in and out, while stones around the edge provide hiding places.

Pond life

A variety of pond plants will create wildlife habitat, add visual interest and maintain the health of the water. Some aquatic plants are sold in basket containers that can be placed directly in the pond. The mesh enables water to circulate around the roots while helping prevent the plants from spreading and taking over.

A wide array of plants are available that thrive in differing depths of water. You should also choose varieties best suited to the size of the pond, as some species grow vigorously.

Submerged aquatic pondweeds help oxygenate the water and popular species include **Hornwort** and **Spiked Water Milfoil**. Floating surface plants like **Frogbit** and waterlilies provide shade for wildlife that seeks to remain out of view from potential predators. Emergent flowering plants in the shallows, such as **Flowering Rush**, attract pollinators and also enable dragonfly larvae to clamber above the pond surface to hatch. Marginal plants suited to the damp edges offer floral interest and natural cover for wildlife, including **Water Mint**, **Marsh Marigold** and **Water Forget-me-not**.

A small water feature is not only attractive, but also provides a home for nature.

▲ Ponds generally require little maintenance, apart from removing dead leaves and excess vegetation.

◀ A Broad-bodied Chaser dragonfly and Great Pond Snail.

Fish are best avoided if you want to maximise wildlife returns, given they will snaffle up larvae, tadpoles and insect life.

Ponds shouldn't need much maintenance, though excess weed can be removed – and should initially be piled at the water's edge to allow any animals trapped within to escape back into the pond. Algae problems may be tackled by adding netted bundles of barley straw, which produce natural chemicals that combat algal growth.

REPTILES AND AMPHIBIANS 53

Common Lizard

Encounters with **Common Lizards** on a hot and sunny walk can be fairly fleeting. A rustling sound alerts you to something moving beside the path, followed by the sight of a thin tail disappearing into the undergrowth.

But if you are lucky enough to get a good view, they are attractively patterned reptiles. Around 10–15cm long and mainly brown, they have light and dark markings running down the slim body and tail.

Colouring can vary, with some individuals being particularly dark, gingery or olive-green. Greenish colouring may confuse people into thinking they have spotted a **Green Lizard** – however this larger species does not occur naturally in mainland Britain. The male **Sand Lizard** (*below*) has bright green sides, but this is a rare British species of heathland and dunes, mainly in Dorset, Surrey and Hampshire.

Common Lizards are found in a range of open habitats, including heaths, grassy scrub, commons, chalk downland, woodland rides and moorland, along with railway embankments, quarries and industrial brownfield sites. This is a hardy species, able to survive at high altitudes and latitudes, and is found right across northern Europe and central Asia.

They bask in the sun to warm up, on rocks, walls, logs or posts close to cover. If disturbed they will dart into the undergrowth, but eventually emerge again and often carry on soaking up the sun's warmth in the same spot, so patience pays when watching them.

British reptiles

Reptiles are seldom easy to spot, tending to keep a low profile and being quick to disappear from view when they detect potential danger.

We have six native reptiles in Britain: three kinds of lizard and three snakes. The **Sand Lizard** (*right*) and **Smooth Snake** are rare species, found at scattered heathland and coastal dune sites. The other four species, featured in these pages, are all fairly common and widespread.

Lizards and snakes are often described as cold-blooded. Strictly speaking they are 'ectothermic', relying on external sources of heat to raise their body temperature. Thermoregulation behaviour, such as basking in the sun or on warm rocks, or seeking out shade in hot weather, means they can maintain their body at a steady temperature. However, in winter they are unable

Common Lizards eat a range of small prey, such as insects and spiders. But they also feature on the menu of predators, including birds and cats. If caught they possess the ability to shed their tail – a muscular contraction causing it to sever along a fracture line near the base. The abandoned tail continues to wriggle, potentially distracting the predator while the lizard makes its escape. It will eventually grow a new tail, though the replacement is shorter in length than the original (*below*).

Like our other reptiles, Common Lizards hibernate in winter, tucked away beneath logs, rocks and leaf litter or underground.

Common Lizards are not as common as they once were and have been in decline over recent decades.

Breeding behaviour

Common Lizards emerge from hibernation early in spring – the males in advance of females. Their worn old skin is sloughed off and when females emerge the males compete for mating rights.

To copulate, the male grasps a female with his jaws, and it is believed males with larger heads are more successful in fending off rivals and successfully mating.

Female Common Lizards incubate fertilised eggs within their body (*below*) and give birth to live young. The young are born within the thin membrane of the egg capsule which sustained them inside the mother's body, and quickly break free.

remain active and are forced to bernate.

On hot summer days these usive and well-camouflaged ptiles can be harder to view given ey are full of energy and alert to

disturbance. Intermittent sunshine is often best, such as a sunny spell after a light shower, as the cooling effect of the rain means reptiles need to bask in the sun to warm up again.

REPTILES AND AMPHIBIANS 55

Slow Worm

It may not be particularly fast moving, but whatever the name suggests, this is definitely no worm. And it is not a snake either – even though it resembles one.

The **Slow Worm** is in fact a legless lizard and totally harmless. And it is probably our most frequently encountered reptile, given that it is widespread and can be found in rural and urban gardens and allotments.

Slow Worms grow to more than 30cm in length. Their smooth, cylindrical bodies have a metallic sheen that varies in colour from golden-brown to brass or copper.

The belly and flanks of a female (*above*) are dark, and they often have a pencil-thin line of black running down the centre of the back. Smaller males (*below*) are greyer, more uniform in colour and are light underneath. Occasionally individuals are attractively speckled with tiny blue dots on their upperside.

Like our other reptiles, Slow Worms need to absorb the warmth of the sun, either directly or indirectly, to maintain their body temperature. However, they tend not to bask in the open. Instead, you are most likely to find Slow Worms resting under coverings exposed

Climate challenge for reptiles

Climate change is likely to present both opportunities and challenges for our reptile populations.

Warming temperatures may enable some species to spread more widely, potentially enabling southerly residents to shift northwards. **Grass Snakes** could gain ground in Scotland, for example. However, changing environmental conditions are expected to make some existing habitats unsuitable, while fragmented landscapes hinder

56 REPTILES AND AMPHIBIANS

Escape trick

If grabbed by a predator or handled roughly, a Slow Worm will shed its tail to escape – a behaviour characteristic of many lizards (*see also: Common Lizard, pages 54–55*). A new tail grows back over time, though it is shorter than the original.

A large proportion of adult Slow Worms have at some point lost and regrown their tail when escaping from predators. As a result, you are quite likely to come across individuals with stumpy, rather than elongated, tail ends.

The replacement tail cannot be shed, so it is an escape trick they are only able to perform once.

to the sun, such as matting or wooden planks on the ground. A section of old carpet on top of a compost heap, or a sheet of corrugated iron in a sunny spot amid undergrowth, provides an ideal warm and sheltered refuge under which they may congregate.

During winter, Slow Worms hibernate in disused burrows or beneath vegetation, and emerge in spring when they mate. Females carrying young become noticeably enlarged around the middle and give birth in late summer to live young, in clutches of around a dozen.

Slow Worms eat a range of invertebrates, including slugs, spiders and earthworms. Compost heaps are a good source of prey, while the rotting plant matter also generates warmth – and their smooth legless bodies enable them to burrow into the soft compost to hunt and hide.

Slow Worms that avoid starvation or predation can be surprisingly long-lived – one individual kept at Copenhagen Zoo was reportedly at least 54 years old when it died.

reptiles from dispersing to new areas.

Milder winters may have a detrimental effect by reducing hibernation length and increasing activity at a time when there is less food available, resulting in individuals depleting vital energy reserves.

Adders, for example, have now been reported as active during every month of the year in Europe – potentially making them vulnerable at times when they should be hibernating (*left*).

In addition, more extreme weather resulting from climate change, such as flash floods or droughts that lead to heathland fires in protected areas, could directly impact reptile numbers. Rare species such as the **Smooth Snake** are put at particular risk by the loss or damage of precious heathland habitat (*right*).

The impacts of a changing climate on prey species and predators will also have knock-on effects on the survival of our reptiles. And sea level rises could affect coastal populations.

Grass Snake

The **Grass Snake** is the largest of our three native species of snake, growing to well over a metre in length. Yet despite its size, the Grass Snake is harmless – and timid, tending to keep out of sight.

Sleek and attractively marked, Grass Snakes are typically grey-green or olive-green, although some may have a brownish tone. Their sides are marked with black vertical bars. Most noticeable of all is a distinctive black-and-yellow collar just behind the head, which helps identify them in an instant. They lack the **Adder**'s dark zigzag down the back (see page 60).

Grass Snakes are found in a range of lowland habitats in England and Wales, ranging from woodland glades, field margins, rough grassland and heathland to rail embankments, golf courses and large gardens. They feed on a variety of prey – particularly fish and amphibians, so tend to inhabit areas with wetlands, lakes or ponds and are good swimmers. They have tiny, backward-pointing teeth to grasp prey, which is swallowed whole and alive.

Like our other reptiles, Grass Snakes hibernate in winter, tucked away under logs or in mammal burrows, and emerge ahead of the spring breeding season. While Adders give birth to live young, Grass Snakes lay clutches of leathery-

Our rarest snake

Of our trio of native snake species, the **Smooth Snake** is by far the rarest of the bunch. Shorter than the Grass Snake and slimmer than the Adder, it is a species of heathlands and confined to a few scattered sites in southern England, in particular Dorset.

This secretive species is greyish-brown and lacks the Adder's dark zigzag along the back and the yellow-and-black collar of the Grass Snake. Its dotted body

Sunny refuge

Grass Snakes are shy animals, but may be chanced across basking in the sun to warm up in the morning or while hunting beside lakes and ponds.

One way of observing them is to place a sheet of corrugated iron or black matting in a sunny vegetated spot close to a pond. By absorbing the sun's heat, these coverings provide an ideal sheltered refuge beneath which reptiles can warm up while staying hidden from view.

Take care when lifting the sheet in case it has also attracted a basking Adder, and replace it gently to avoid crushing any wildlife present.

kinned white eggs (*left*) during the summer rotting vegetation. The warmth emitted by he decomposing plant matter incubates the eveloping young, which hatch after 2–3 months. ompost heaps in gardens and allotments provide ideal locations.

Grass Snakes are quick to retreat into cover if they detect danger. When threatened they may play dead, rolling onto their back with their mouth open. And if caught by a predator – or handled – they can eject a foul-smelling liquid from their anal gland, which acts as a deterrent to capture.

The Grass Snake (*Natrix natrix*) has a wide range across Europe. A scientific study in 2017 determined that those native to Britain and western Europe are genetically distinct from Grass Snakes living east of the River Rhine. As a result, our Grass Snake has been reclassified as a separate species, with the scientific name *Natrix helvetica*, common name **Barred Grass Snake**.

arkings are not particularly ye-catching, however its head has unique chocolate-coloured patch n the top in the rough shape a heart and it also has a dark orizontal stripe through the eye.

The scales are smooth to e touch, hence the name, hich allows it to glide through eathland heather, in which it asks and hunts.

The Smooth Snake is not enomous but instead grabs ey, such as lizards and small ammals, with tough little teeth and wraps itself around its victim like a constrictor to prevent escape.

To stand a chance of seeing this protected snake, the UK's rarest native reptile, you will need to accompany a licensed expert on an organised survey at an established site.

Adder

Of the UK's three native species of snake the **Adder**, also known as the Viper, is the only one with a venomous bite.

Adders are mostly found in open habitats, such as heathland, moorland, along sea cliffs and woodland glades, road and rail embankments. They are thick-bodied, grey or brown in colour, with red eyes, and have a dark zigzag running the length of their back. This bold patterning is distinctive and enables them to be distinguished in an instant from our other snakes.

The sexes can be told apart by the tone of their colouring. The male is paler, with a silvery-grey body and charcoal-black zigzag pattern along the back. Females are larger and browner – the body looks almost tea-stained or has a coppery hue, topped with a chocolate-brown zigzag. Occasional 'melanistic' individuals are recorded that are virtually black in appearance.

You might imagine that a dry summer's day is the optimum time to encounter Adders. However, in warm conditions these reptiles are active and alert to approaching footsteps. Instead, they are more easily observed when they emerge from hibernation in the spring, sluggish after their winter slumber. At this time of year they rest in the sunshine, close to cover, for prolonged periods of the day to raise their body temperature.

Adders engage in sunbathing behaviour whenever they have cooled down – such as after a rain shower – and often flatten their body to increase the surface area and absorb as much heat as possible. Even then they are extremely well camouflaged and easily missed, coiled up or stretched out motionless amid bracken and long grass. They are sensitive to movement and

Adder bites

Whether you like Adders or find them sinister, few British animals make for such attention-grabbing encounters. Perhaps this is partly because we don't tend to come across them often; Adders do their level best not to be noticed and to keep out of our way.

Adders are venomous, and their bites are potentially serious. However, they are not aggressive, preferring to hide when disturbed.

Regardless of size or age, Adders

may bite if they feel threatened or are handled or accidentally trodden on. Several dozen people are bitten every year in Britain – a significant proportion resulting from trying to pick up the snake.

The last person in Britain to die from an Adder bite was in 1975.

Dance of the Adders

During the colder months, Adders hibernate underground, such as in a disused Rabbit burrow or beneath a tree stump. These sites may be occupied communally every winter.

The males stir earliest in spring, and generally stick close to home, soaking up the sun's warmth in March and April when the weather permits. They slough off their old skin, giving them a fresh appearance with well-defined markings.

During the spring breeding season, rival males battle with each other in a sinuous test of strength known as the 'dance of the Adders' – intertwining with heads raised and endeavouring to force the opponent to the ground. Females give birth to live young in late summer.

vibrations and quickly disappear if they sense danger.

Adders pick up scents using their forked tongue, 'tasting' the air, and feed on rodents, lizards and ground-nesting birds. Unlike mammals, reptiles do not burn up large quantities of calories maintaining their body temperature, so can eat less frequently.

While reptiles are warmth-loving animals, the Adder is well adapted to cold conditions, and is found in northern Scotland and even above the Arctic Circle in Scandinavia.

Statistically, on a country walk, cattle and lightning are far more dangerous than Adders in terms of fatalities.

Having said that, we should not be complacent. While the majority of bites are not life-threatening, they can lead to health complications and are especially dangerous for children. Anyone bitten should remain calm, keep the affected limb as still as possible and dial 999 to seek immediate medical attention.

Inquisitive dogs are also at risk of being bitten and immediate veterinary attention should be sought, while keeping the injured dog as calm as possible.

REPTILES AND AMPHIBIANS

Butterflies

Red Admiral

If you asked someone to name a butterfly, the chances are they would say **Red Admiral**. Its aristocratic title is arguably the most well known of all our butterflies. Added to which, this boldly marked species is a common sight in parks and gardens, as well as the wider countryside.

The Red Admiral is a large and strong-flying butterfly with distinctive patterning – a unique contrasting combination of black, red and white. The wings are velvety black, with a band of orange-red across the front wings and around the edge of the hindwings. At the front wing-tips it has blotches of white.

The Red Admiral is widespread and common in Britain. Its abundance depends upon large influxes from continental Europe in late spring and early summer, whose offspring boost overall numbers.

Only a small proportion survive our winters, chiefly in southern Britain, where milder conditions enable them to successfully hibernate, tucked away in sheltered nooks and crannies during the colder months. Climate change is expected to result in increasing numbers enduring through winter.

Butterflies in Britain

Nothing matches the joy of sunny weather more than butterflies, animating bright days with their fluttering flight and flashes of colour.

Delicate insects of exquisite beauty, they have understandably won a place in our hearts, lifting the spirits and providing a source of inspiration and natural wonder.

When it comes to identification, our 59 regular species provide the perfect mix for beginner and

Heath Fritillary butterflies (*above*) and a male Common Blue (*right*).

Identifying species

Identifying butterflies can be tricky, as the variations in colouring that separate one kind from another may be subtle. Added to which, males and females of the same species can look different.

And you don't just need to view the neatly spread upperwings – the patterning on the underside provides as many clues when it comes to putting a name to a species, especially as some butterfly species always close their wings whenever they land.

Taking photos certainly helps – if the butterfly is obliging enough to settle close by – enabling the observer to later check the markings in detail against photos in a guide.

Overwintering adults occasionally take to the wing on sunny days, even in November and December, making for surprise sightings that feel very much 'out of season'.

In some years, Red Admirals are extremely common, flitting between nectar-rich summer blooms, such as Bramble blossom.

During autumn they stock up their energy reserves by feeding on the sweet juice of windfall apples, plums and other fruit. The fermenting juice of rotting fruit can result in butterflies becoming slightly drunk! These dozy individuals are easy to approach and even lift up on a finger.

Some Red Admirals fly south across the Channel before the onset of freezing winter weather.

Red Admiral females lay their eggs on a variety of plants that suit the appetites of their caterpillars, in particular nettles. The dark caterpillars hide within a folded leaf when not feeding.

The Red Admiral is not the only admiral among our butterflies. The **White Admiral** (*left*) is a handsome summer butterfly of sunny woodland glades in southern and central England. It has white bands – instead of red – across its dark wings and typically feeds on Bramble flowers.

expert alike – ranging from a number of common and boldly marked butterflies, to a host of more localised and harder-to-identify varieties.

They include groupings such as the so-called 'aristocrats' – large, colourful and fast-flying species like the Red Admiral and scarce **Purple Emperor**; the fritillary butterflies with their chequered markings of orange and black; the butterflies sporting dazzling upperwings; white butterflies and brown butterflies that are a familiar sight in gardens and meadows; as well as the moth-like skippers and striking little hairstreaks.

While butterflies are generally active in fine weather, the time of year when they are on the wing varies from species to species. Some flutter by on sunny days whatever the month, while others have more distinct flight seasons in spring or summer. It pays to know when, as well as where, species are likely to be found.

Small Tortoiseshell

The **Small Tortoiseshell** is an attractive resident butterfly and a familiar sight in spring and summer.

This widespread species can be identified by its marmalade-orange wings marked with black-and-gold blocks along the front, and blue fringes around the outer edges.

Close up, with wings spread as it basks in the sun, it is a glorious-looking butterfly, and will readily visit gardens in rural or urban areas to feed on the nectar of flowers.

When conditions are favourable the Small Tortoiseshell can manage at least two broods in a year, as one generation successfully completes its life cycle and produces the next set of offspring. This can result in an abundance of the butterflies in late summer and early autumn.

However, the Small Tortoiseshell has good years and bad, and its fortunes have fluctuated over recent decades.

Small Tortoiseshells hibernate to get through harsh weather during the colder months, tucked away in natural holes and hollows, as well as in built structures with a cool and constant temperature such as tunnels, garden sheds and attics. It means the adults get a head start come spring, emerging from their hideaways ready to breed early in the season.

Males and females are identical in appearance. However, males may be identified in the afternoon as they become territorial, chasing rivals from their chosen patch and courting females – which they do by drumming their antennae on the female's hindwings.

In late summer and autumn, the butterflies seek out the nectar of a range of flowers, including

Butterfly life cycle

Most female butterflies lay their tiny eggs either singly or in batches on the specific plants upon which their caterpillars feed.

Once the eggs hatch, the caterpillars that emerge dedicate themselves to eating. They will shed their outer skin several times during this larval stage as they grow.

The caterpillar eventually turns into a chrysalis, with a tough outer casing that is usually

well camouflaged. During this pupation stage, the miracle of metamorphosis takes place as the cellular soup within rearranges itself into a butterfly.

The adult butterfly emerges from the cramped confines of the chrysalis and pumps fluid into the veins of its crumpled wings to enable them to gradually expand before it takes flight.

The adult body comprises a head section, a thorax in the

Migrant visitors

Most of the butterflies found in Britain are resident, but a small number are migratory. They cross the English Channel from continental Europe to breed, though are not adapted to survive here during winter. Species include the **Clouded Yellow**, **Red Admiral** and **Painted Lady**, which may be present in large numbers during summer as their offspring take to the wing.

Rare migrants also turn up occasionally, particularly in coastal areas of southern England. They include species such as the **Long-tailed Blue** and **Camberwell Beauty**, from Europe, and, incredibly, the large and strong-flying **Monarch** butterfly, from North America.

Monarch (*left*) and Camberwell Beauty (*right*) butterflies are rare visitors to the British Isles.

Verbena (*left*), topping up their energy reserves in preparation for hibernation.

The caterpillars feed on nettles – as do those of the **Red Admiral**, **Peacock** and **Comma**. The perfect reason to leave a patch of nettles growing in your garden.

The Small Tortoiseshell has a very similar-looking larger relative – the **Large Tortoiseshell** – which was once common in Britain. It became extinct in this country by the middle of the twentieth century, though is still widespread in Europe. There are occasional sightings, mainly in south-east England, of individuals that may have flown over the Channel, and in recent years these records have increased.

middle (which the wings and legs are attached to), and a long abdomen at the tail end that contains the digestive tract and reproductive organs.

Adult butterflies feed on the nectar of flowers, giving them the energy they require to fly and find mates. A few woodland butterflies also drink tree sap and honeydew secreted by aphids.

Adult butterflies may live for days, weeks or even months depending on the species.

BUTTERFLIES 67

Peacock

Few British species are as stunning as the **Peacock** butterfly.

When its wings are folded, showing only the dark undersides, it resembles a dead leaf (*right*) – perfect camouflage when at rest or during winter when it remains dormant for months on end in natural cavities and outbuildings and needs to avoid attracting attention to itself.

But when it opens its wings, the Peacock becomes a thing of dazzling splendour.

Most spectacular are the symmetrical eye-spots on both fore- and hindwings, designed to startle predators – each highlighted with glittering touches of iridescent blue. The wing patterning also contrasts areas of black with sweeps of rusty red, flecks of gold, flashes of yellow and swirling brushstrokes of white and grey.

Best of all, this glorious-looking butterfly is a species that everyone can enjoy, being a garden regular. It often visits purple-flowered Buddleia, which is known as the 'butterfly bush'.

Buddleia is an invasive non-native species, having been introduced to Britain from China in

Surviving winter

The colder months of the year present a challenge for butterflies, given they depend upon warm temperatures and flower nectar to remain active.

Some species pass through winter at the egg stage of their life cycle; others as dormant caterpillars or in the form of a chrysalis. A handful of our butterflies – Peacock, **Brimstone, Comma, Red Admiral** and **Small Tortoiseshell** – overwinter as adults, tucked away in tree hollow and outbuildings or amid dense foliage.

Peacock and Small Tortoiseshe butterflies may even seek refuge inside houses and garages. If foun they are best left in a cool place to see out the winter or released outside on a suitably warm and dry day.

Our overwintering butterflies typically feed up on nectar or the sweet juices of windfall fruit in la

Camouflage

Butterflies that hibernate through winter, such as the Peacock, rely on camouflage to avoid drawing attention to themselves.

While their conspicuous upperwings may be gloriously patterned, the undersides – visible at rest – are dark and drab. The mottled patterning resembles that of a dried leaf – a tatty one in the case of the Comma's ragged outline.

With some species, including various blue butterflies, females are less brightly coloured than males. When laying eggs, females are vulnerable to predation, so it pays to keep a low profile.

A number of our butterflies have muted markings and dull colouring which blends in with their surroundings – among them the aptly named **Dingy Skipper** (*left*).

he late 1800s. It has become widely naturalised in his country, but there are many alternative native ants that are popular with Peacock butterflies, cluding Marjoram, Betony, bluebells, teasels, istles and dandelions.

In spring, Peacock butterfly males are rritorial, choosing a sunny spot from which ey see off rival males and pursue females. The males lay their eggs in May on the underside of ttle leaves, and the caterpillars are distinctive oking, being black with white speckles and ack spines (*right*).

When threatened the Peacock butterfly flashes en its wings to reveal its striking eye markings, aring' back at any potential predator. As it does , it also makes an audible hissing sound as its rewings and hindwings rub together – quite an nerving combination!

The Peacock is a strong-flying and widespread sident species that has increased its range rthwards in recent years.

In the annual citizen science survey, the Big Butterfly Count, organised by charity Butterfly Conservation, the Peacock is among the species most spotted by participants. A common butterfly of uncommon beauty.

mmer and autumn to sustain m through the long dormant ase. On mild and sunny winter s some may stir and put in appearance, fluttering around earch of food to top up their rgy reserves.

Those species that hibernate ugh the winter have the longest spans of our butterflies, surviving one year until the next.

ock butterflies seek shelter in er, their folded wings resembling d leaves.

BUTTERFLIES

Comma

This handsome butterfly could be confused with a **Small Tortoiseshell** or even a fritillary butterfly, given that it has orangey upperwings marked with bold blocks of dark patterning. However, the scalloped wing edges that give it a ragged outline are distinctive.

With wings closed, the dark brown underside resembles a dead leaf, tattered and torn. This provides excellent camouflage, which is especially important as the **Comma** is one of a handful of British butterflies that hibernate as adults during winter. It is secretive at this time of year and lies dormant amid woodland vegetation, on branches or in tree hollows.

Early in spring, as temperatures rise, Commas become active again and are among the first butterflies of the season to take to the wing. They often bask in the warmth of the sun with wings spread, revealing their attractive colouring.

Males establish territories along woodland edges and in glades where there is plenty of sunshine. They may patrol up and down, typically returning to a favoured perch as they wait for a female to pass by.

Females will mate with several males before laying their eggs. The small greenish eggs are laid singly on the leaf of the larval foodplant, which is predominantly nettles. The dark caterpillars that hatch take several weeks to fully mature, moultin[g] several times as they grow. They are quite bizarre-looking, with orange-and-white patches on the spiny upperside. This colouring is believed to act a[s] an ingenious and off-putting form of camouflage (*see panel below*).

Butterfly caterpillars

The caterpillars of our butterflies come in all shapes and sizes.

Being soft-bodied they are vulnerable to being eaten, especially by birds. To minimise the risk many have camouflaged colouring, blending in with their surroundings. Quite a number are as green as the leaves upon which they feed.

Some deter potential predators by advertising the fact that they are distasteful with bright colours or a covering of spines or hairs. The

orangey-brown caterpillar of the Comma (*left*) has a long white pa[tch] on its back so as to resemble a b[ird] dropping! As caterpillars grow, th[ey] shed their outer skin several time[s] before reaching full size.

Feeding at night reduces the chances of predation, and the caterpillars of some species hide within leaves or live communall[y] under silken webs.

A variety of foodplants may sustain various caterpillars, but butterfly species can be particul[ar]

The Comma chrysalis is mottled brown and resembles a withered leaf (*top right*). This pupation stage lasts around a fortnight before the winged adult emerges.

If conditions are favourable, the spring offspring of breeding Commas that develop into adults will themselves produce another brood in late summer. These second-generation butterflies are slightly darker in appearance. They gorge on flower nectar and the sweet juices of autumn windfall fruit before hibernating.

The Comma takes its unusual name from the punctuation term – it has a small white comma-shaped mark on the hind underwings, visible when its wings are closed (*below*).

Changing fortunes

The British population of the Comma butterfly has had its ups and downs over the last couple of centuries.

Once widespread, numbers of Commas declined sharply in the late 1800s until it became a real scarcity. It is believed this may have been due to a reduction in the commercial growing of hops, upon which its caterpillars feed.

Fortunately, Comma caterpillars also eat nettles, which are far more plentiful. In recent decades numbers have been on an upward trend. The species has expanded its range throughout England and Wales since the 1960s and is pressing north into Scotland.

cky. Caterpillars of the **Small** ue butterfly, for example, only ed on a low-growing plant called dney Vetch. Nettles are eaten by ange of caterpillars, including ose of **Red Admiral**, **Peacock**, all Tortoiseshell and Comma tterflies. And, as any gardener l know, the caterpillars of the rge White butterfly (also known the Cabbage White) will eat e leaves of cabbages, kale and sturtiums (*right*).

BUTTERFLIES

Painted Lady

The **Painted Lady** is a butterfly that can be abundant some years and less common in others, the reason being that this fast-flying wanderer is a visitor that does not reside in Britain year-round. Instead it migrates, sometimes long distances, from countries further south, multiplying and spreading in favourable conditions.

In good summers, vast numbers flood into Britain, adorning patches of thistles alongside our resident species, while in poorer years this migrant species becomes something of a scarcity.

In terms of identification, the engagingly named Painted Lady is similar in size and shape to the **Red Admiral** (*see page 64*) and has distinctive, complicated patterning of black and white on a pinkish-orange background, which can fade as the adults age.

Painted Ladies can be seen throughout the warmer months across Britain, but perish as temperatures plummet in winter. It is believed some make a return journey across the Channel in autumn to escape our winter frosts.

Occasionally a number are spotted during the colder months, having flown here on warm winds from the south – even from as far away as northern Africa. In spring and summer, those Painted Ladies that have arrived in Britain mate and multiply, laying their eggs primarily on thistles.

Growing caterpillars create a silk tent around the leaves they are feeding on, which helps protect them from predators.

The wings of some adult butterflies can be particularly worn and torn – the result of life on the move, damage inflicted by birds, or from

Big Butterfly Count

The Big Butterfly Count is run every summer by the charity Butterfly Conservation. The UK-wide 'citizen science' survey – similar to the RSPB's winter Big Garden Birdwatch – provides a snapshot of how our species are faring.

Launched in 2010, it has become the world's biggest survey of butterflies, with tens of thousands of people taking part. Not only does it reveal gains and losses in butterfly populations, but the fortunes of these pollinators also shed light on the wider health of ecosystems and the environment.

Participants are invited to count the butterflies they see in their garden, local park or the wider countryside during a 15-minute period. The survey is held in July and August – the three-week timespan increasing the odds of those taking part enjoying at least one window of sunny weather when butterflies are on the wing.

Butterfly Conservation also publishes a 'state of the nation'

Millions on the move

Mass migrations of butterflies such as the Painted Lady have been tracked in recent years by radar.

Researchers monitoring the passage of flying insects in the skies over southern England have estimated that some 3.5 trillion invertebrates sweep into the country every spring. Migrating species range from aphids and hoverflies to beetles, moths and butterflies.

Travelling by day and night, many at altitudes of more than a kilometre above ground, their combined biomass can be measured in the thousands of tonnes.

In the autumn, vast numbers of flying insects are on the move once again, this time heading southwards.

feeding amid the prickles of flowering Brambles and thistles.

The Painted Lady is one of the most widespread butterflies in the world, being found on every continent except South America and Antarctica. A powerful flyer with strong migratory instincts, it can undertake remarkable long-distance journeys and has even been recorded in Iceland.

As these butterflies push north through Europe to Britain in spring they reproduce along the way, with one generation after another creating rolling waves of migrating individuals. The restless Painted Lady flitting around your garden may have travelled hundreds of kilometres before dropping by and settling on a flower to refuel on nectar.

assessment of the UK's 59 species of breeding butterfly every five or so years. *The State of the UK's Butterflies 2022* revealed 80 per cent of species had declined since the 1970s – particularly affected were 'specialist' butterflies with precise, rather than general, habitat requirements. Such widespread decreases in our butterfly populations are a 'huge cause for concern', the charity said.

BUTTERFLIES 73

Gardening for butterflies

Our gardens can act as sanctuaries for nature on a small scale. And also on a large scale, when you consider that the total land area of private gardens across Britain is larger than all the nation's nature reserves combined.

By including a few nectar-rich plants in sunny areas of a backyard plot, you are sure to attract a diversity of flying insects.

Butterflies require flowers which provide them with the sugary fuel that powers their active lives. To multiply, they also need a range of other plants upon which their caterpillars feed.

The more on offer, the greater the number of butterflies and variety of species you are likely to attract and sustain from one generation to the next. And our butterflies certainly need all the help they can get, given that the majority of British species are suffering ongoing declines in numbers and distribution.

Floral delights

Adult butterflies feed on sweet high-energy drinks, such as nectar, aphid honeydew and the juice of windfall fruits. They suck it up through their proboscis, which acts like a long straw.

Flowers produce nectar to entice insects that aid pollination, and a wide variety of flowering plants are visited by butterflies.

Best-known among them is **Buddleia**, also known as the 'butterfly bush' because its purple blooms are a magnet for these insects. But this non-native plant is fast growing and highly invasive. Thankfully, there are many other less invasive plants that are proven to attract butterflies to your garden.

Verbena is a favourite with butterflies, producing small clusters of nectar-rich purple flowers in summer and autumn. The plant thrives in sunshine and has a long flowering season, attracting not only butterflies but also day-flying moths.

The perennial sun-loving herb **Marjoram** is a winner with butterflies, hoverflies and bees, which are drawn in numbers to its bushy mounds of little flowers in summer.

Aromatic **Lavender**, which is easy to grow in well-drained soil, not only looks pretty, but its summer flowers attract butterflies. As do the pink florets of the autumn-flowering **Sedum** and the light blue flowers of **Nepeta**, also known as catmint.

Wildflower plants to consider include **Common Knapweed** and **Field Scabious**. **Bluebells** and **Bramble** blossom are also attractive to butterflies while **Ivy** offers an important source of nectar late in the year.

Ideally you will have a range of plants that bloom at different times to provide floral interest throughout the seasons.

▲ Flowering Marjoram attracts a variety of butterflies, such as the Holly Blue.

▶ A patch of wildflowers, including Field Scabious, pays dividends with pollinators.

Caterpillar foodplants

Butterflies are not only drawn to garden flowers, but also to plants upon which they can lay their eggs.

They choose such plants based on the specific diet of their caterpillars, and some species are fussier than others. Dozens of different foodplants sustain the populations of our 59 resident butterflies, ranging from wildflowers and grasses to the leaves of trees and shrubs. Gardens can be limited in terms of the range of breeding butterflies they are able to host, but may still provide for a few common species.

Once butterfly eggs hatch, the small larvae that emerge have big appetites and grow rapidly. These very hungry caterpillars may not all be popular with gardeners – especially those of the **Large White** (Cabbage White), which eat the leaves of brassicas and nasturtiums. But not all butterfly caterpillars are troublesome guests – and a number have a taste for foliage we might consider weeds.

An excellent foodplant is the humble **Stinging Nettle**, which sustains the caterpillars of some of our most attractive garden butterflies, including the **Peacock**, **Small Tortoiseshell**, **Red Admiral** and **Comma**. A patch of nettles in a sheltered, sunny corner will reward the wildlife-friendly gardener when the adult butterflies take to the wing, adding a dash of colour and movement to a garden scene.

◄ Thistles are among the foodplants favoured by Painted Lady caterpillars.

Holly Blue caterpillars feed on **Holly**, as the name suggests, and **Ivy**, while those of the **Painted Lady** are particularly partial to thistles. The caterpillars of the **Small Copper** butterfly dine out on **Common Sorrel**; **Brimstone** larvae eat **Buckthorn** leaves, and **Orange-tip** caterpillars are keen on **Charlock**, **Cuckooflower** and **Garlic Mustard**, among other plants.

If room allows, creating a small garden meadow by leaving a patch of lawn uncut or by sowing a wildflower mix can pay dividends in terms of natural interest. A mini-meadow may attract breeding **Meadow Brown**, **Gatekeeper** and **Large Skipper** butterflies, whose caterpillars eat various grasses.

Fruits of the season

In the autumn, fallen ripe fruits, including **plums**, **pears** and **apples**, provide a valuable source of food for butterflies that overwinter as adults.

Leaving windfall fruit on the ground will help species, such as the Red Admiral and Comma, to prepare for hibernation. Impressive numbers of butterflies may gather beneath fruit trees, taking advantage of the energy-rich juices of the rotting fruit.

▼ Ripe blackberries provide sugary sustenance for butterflies such as the Comma.

BUTTERFLIES 75

Brimstone

The male **Brimstone**, with its butter-coloured wings, is believed to be the original inspiration for the word 'butterfly'.

Only the males are this glorious yellow and eye-catching in flight; the females are much paler.

When Brimstones land to feed or rest they keep their large wings closed. The creamy-greenish undersides of the folded wings have the appearance of fresh leaves, with prominent veins and pointed tips, providing excellent camouflage (*right*).

Many butterflies count their lives in days and weeks rather than months. However, Brimstones are remarkably long-lived and able to survive from one summer to the next. They are among a handful of species that endure our colder months in a dormant state as adult butterflies, sheltering from the worst of the winter weather in natural or humanmade hollows and hideaways.

Once temperatures rise, Brimstones emerge from hibernation and can be seen on the wing from early spring. They are strong fliers and roam widely in open woodlands, grassland, along hedgerows and in gardens. Males and females may be spotted in spring spiralling upwards together in courtship flight before mating.

The species is widely distributed in England and Wales and has spread in northern counties over recent years, but is only occasionally recorded north of the border in southern Scotland.

Not quite a Brimstone?

The male Brimstone is fairly unmistakable, given its lemon-yellow wings – most noticeable in flight. The only other yellow butterfly with which it could be confused is the **Clouded Yellow** (*right*). This migrant species from the Continent is a regular summer visitor to southern Britain, and in some years is common, particularly along the south coast.

Unlike the Brimstone, the Clouded Yellow's golden wings are edged with black, visible as it passes by in characteristically low flight.

Female Brimstones are such a pale shade of yellowish-green that they might be muddled with the slightly smaller **Large White** butterfly. However, Brimstones have a pointed leaf-like wing shape while the Large White has smooth-edged wings bearing black tips and prominent black dots on the forewings (*see page 78*).

The Brimstone butterfly is not the only 'brimstone' among our flying insects. The **Brimstone Moth** is also bright yellow, but smaller, with brown markings on the front wings (*see page 107*).

76 BUTTERFLIES

Orange-tip

The **Orange-tip** is a member of the same family as white butterflies, but with a difference – the males sport unmistakable bright orange wing-tips. This attractive wedge of tangerine can be spotted even in flight.

Females, on the other hand, lack this colour and look very much like other white butterflies. However, both male and female Orange-tips can be distinguished from other white species at rest when their wings are folded: their hindwings are mottled with camouflage greenish-grey blotching underneath.

The Orange-tip is among the earliest butterflies out and about in spring – a welcome sight given its cheery splashes of wing colour.

Our butterfly species endure winter at differing stages of their life cycle. A few species get through the cold months as hibernating adults, a number overwinter as eggs, the majority as caterpillars (larvae) in a dormant state, and around a dozen species at the chrysalis (pupa) stage of development. The Orange-tip butterfly adopts the latter strategy – its well-camouflaged chrysalis, attached to a stem and shaped like a thorn, survives winter in a state of suspended animation (*above*). Once temperatures rise in spring, life processes are stirred back into action, development is completed and the adult butterfly emerges from the chrysalis.

This is a widespread butterfly of damp meadow and grassland habitats, and will visit gardens.

Females lay their eggs on a range of plants – but only one per plant, avoiding those which already have an Orange-tip egg on them, the reason being that the caterpillars are cannibalistic and whichever hatches first will eat any other eggs present.

Open and shut case

Some butterflies make identification easy by opening their wings when at rest or feeding – such as the **Peacock** butterfly and **Red Admiral**. With wings spread they almost appear to invite admiration, showing off their striking colours and patterning.

However, a number of butterflies shut their wings as soon as they land, so we only get glimpses of the upper surface in flight. They include the **Brimstone**, **Grayling** and **Green Hairstreak**.

Patterning on the underside of wings can provide useful clues to the identity of a species – for example, helping to distinguish between some fritillary butterflies that have similar chequered orange-and-black markings on their upperwings.

In the case of the Orange-tip, the female (*below*) lacks the male's orange wing-tips and looks almost identical to a **Small White** butterfly. But with wings closed the Orange-tip's underside has greenish mottling, while the Small White underwing is plain.

BUTTERFLIES 77

Large White

White butterflies may lack the ornate patterning and colouring of our most flamboyant species, but are attractive in their own understated way and are a regular sight fluttering around gardens and the wider countryside.

The three most common and widespread species – **Large White**, **Small White** and **Green-veined White** – are not easy to tell apart given they all have white wings marked with dark smudges and spots.

Size is not always a defining factor, despite their names, while the males and females of the same species also have differences between them that can cause confusion.

As a result, many people lump these species together under the term 'cabbage white'.

The Large White is the biggest of the common white butterflies, and not popular with gardeners given the caterpillars devour the leaves of cabbage plants, Brussels sprouts and nasturtiums.

The spread front wings have prominent black tips, extending down the sides, and the underside of the hindwings is creamy-white (*right*).

The female Large White is the bigger of the sexes and an impressive looking butterfly, with solid black dots, as if applied with a marker pen, in the centre of the upperside of the front wings.

The male, on the other hand, is smaller, lacks the dots and is less boldly marked.

Other white butterflies

The common **Small White** butterfly (*left*) has dark tips to its front wings – however this is not as extensive nor as dark as the black around the wing tips of the Large White butterfly. The hindwings of the Small White have pale yellowish undersides, similar to those of its larger relative.

When it comes to distinguishing between Small White sexes it is a case of 'spot' the difference – quite literally. The female has two dark spots on the upperside of her front wings, while the male only has one.

Like the Large White, the caterpillars of this species have an appetite for brassicas, such as cabbages, as well as nasturtiums, and can often be seen fluttering around allotments and garden vegetable beds. Adults in search of nectar are particularly fond of white flowers.

The **Green-veined White** (*right*) is very similar-looking to the Small

Not quite all white?

The **Marbled White** is an eye-catching butterfly of rough grassland and one of a kind in appearance, being our only chequered black-and-white species. However despite its name, it actually belongs to the family of 'brown' butterflies rather than being related to the 'white' species.

The Marbled White is largely found in southern England, though has been gradually extending its range northwards.

This butterfly is on the wing in the summer and most likely to be seen on sunny walks, as it is not a regular garden visitor.

While the Small White butterfly is particularly attracted to white flowers, the Marbled White prefers purple blooms, such as thistles.

Despite the name, male Large Whites could actually be confused with Small White butterflies (*bottom left*). However, the Small White has less extensive black at the tips of the forewings.

Large White caterpillars are fairly distinctive, being black with a yellow stripe down the back and along the sides (*far left*). They feed together in full view and you might think these gregarious grubs easy pickings for hungry birds. However, their colouring signals the fact that they are unpalatable, given they accumulate noxious oils from the plants they eat.

Our resident population of Large Whites may be boosted in summer by migrating butterflies from continental Europe.

While cabbage whites are among Britain's most abundant butterflies, one member of the family is among our rarest: the **Wood White**. Found in scattered locations, this small, delicate-looking species has distinctive rounded wing-tips.

White, with dark wing-tips and a ...ot or two on the open white wings. ...owever, the clue is in the name: it ...an be told apart by the greenish-...rey 'veins' that radiate across the ...nderside of the hindwings – visible ...hen it lands and closes its wings.

This species is widespread and ...ommon in Britain, including ...cotland. It is found across a variety ...f habitats and is a garden regular.

Just like the Large White and ...mall White, the Green-veined White ...as at least two broods of offspring ... a year, in spring and summer.

BUTTERFLIES 79

Meadow Brown

A number of our butterflies tend towards a modest palette of hues when it comes to wing colouring – providing them with excellent camouflage. Among these species are various predominantly brown butterflies.

While arguably not as photogenic as our showier species, they have a subtle beauty of their own, their wings including brushstrokes of orange and grey as well as dark spots that can help with identification.

The **Meadow Brown** is one of our most abundant butterflies, but is easy to overlook given its rather drab appearance.

On the wing in the summer and autumn, the Meadow Brown is mainly found in open grassy areas, where they can be numerous, but also along hedgerows, verges and they can turn up in gardens.

They are unhurried butterflies, often encountered fluttering in a leisurely fashion low

Small Heath

The **Small Heath** (*right*) is an inconspicuous butterfly that tends to flutter low above the ground over short distances – and might even be mistaken for a delicate little moth.

Typically flushed when walking on a sunny summer's day in grassland and heathland habitats or among coastal dunes, the diminutive Small Heath's orangey-brown colouring and ground-hugging behaviour help to identify it.

Its upperwings, with a span of less than 4cm, are light orange – but this is only visible in flight as it closes its wings immediately upon landing. Touching down it shows an eye-spot on the underside of its front wings before hiding this from view behind grey-brown hindwings.

The species is widespread, but numbers have suffered a steep decline over the last half century.

The British Isles are home to several other brown butterflies which are scarce or more localised in distribution. They include the **Wall** butterfly – a fast-flying species of open ground that has suffered a steep decline in numbers. It has light amber

above grasses. The wings are earthy brown, with a dark spot on the forewings that is surrounded by a blaze of orange on females and only a hint of orange on the darker, plainer males. These prominent dark spots are a shared characteristic among our brown butterflies. Situated towards the front of the wing, they resemble eyes and provide a good form of defence.

By flashing their wings to reveal these 'eyes', butterflies may startle and intimidate potential predators. In addition, the eye-spots help divert the attention of an attacker away from the body. A bird may be drawn to peck at the false 'eyes', giving the butterfly a chance of escape with just a torn wing.

The Meadow Brown may be confused with a similar, if slightly smaller species called the **Gatekeeper** (*below*). This more brightly coloured butterfly is an orange-centred chocolate treat, the warm hues in the middle of the wings surrounded with dark brown borders.

The Gatekeeper has quite prominent dark eye-spots on the front of the forewings, each highlighted with double white dots (the Meadow Brown's eyespots usually have just one white dot).

Active in July and August, Gatekeepers are found in the southern half of Britain. Also known as the Hedge Brown, this common species inhabits shrubby, flowery and grassy areas – with or without gates!

Grayling

Strolling along a coast path or through open heathland in late summer, you may come across a fairly large, greyish-brown butterfly that flies up from the ground just ahead, before settling a little further away – and then seemingly disappearing.

The **Grayling** is a master of camouflage. When it lands it immediately closes its wings, tucking its front wings behind mottled hindwings. Not only does it appear smaller – even tilting its folded wings so as not to stand upright – but the wavy grey-and-brown patterning blends in perfectly with the bare earth or stones upon which it usually settles.

The Gatekeeper is similar to the Meadow Brown, but with far more orange on both front and rear wings.

patterning resembling that of a fritillary and likes to bask on rocks and walls, as the name suggests. The **Scotch Argus** is mainly found in Scotland and looks similar to the Meadow Brown, though has several spots on its sooty-brown wings.

The Small Heath butterfly settles with its wings closed, revealing a dark eye-spot on the underside of its orangey forewing.

Speckled Wood

Take a walk in a woodland on a warm summer's day and you are sure to come across this common butterfly, flying along the shaded edges of the path or spiralling in shafts of sunlight.

As the name suggests, the **Speckled Wood** favours woodlands, especially those with dappled light – which mirrors the dappled lighter patches on its brown wings. They can also be seen in gardens and along hedgerows.

Males are territorial, patrolling their stretch of habitat and guarding sunny spots in woodland glades. They can be seen chasing away intruders, typically rising in corkscrew formation with their opponents – like a double helix of battling butterflies.

The Speckled Wood may be recognised, even in flight, by the creamy patches and spots covering the chocolate-brown wings, and can be encountered from spring through until autumn.

The butterflies feed on the nectar of a variety of wildflowers, but also drink 'honeydew' – a sweet liquid excreted by aphids as they tap into the sap of plants. A number of other woodland butterflies also exploit this source of sugary liquid found on tree leaves.

The Speckled Wood is unusual among our butterflies in that it may spend winter in either the caterpillar or chrysalis stages of its life cycle.

Ringlet

This lovely dark brown butterfly of mid to late summer is found in lush grasslands, along hedgerows and in woodland glades, flying low and feeding on Brambles and other flowers.

Ringlets have a distinctive weak, bouncy flight and can be observed at close quarters over grasses. Unlike many butterflies they also fly on dull days – their dark colouring readily absorbing heat and helping them to warm up quickly in overcast conditions.

The Ringlet can be told apart from other brown butterflies, such as the similar **Meadow Brown** (see page 80), by its uniform velvety-brown wings, which have a thin fringe of white. At rest, the underside of the wings have telltale groups of distinctive circular spots – the 'rings' that give it its name.

The caterpillars feed on a range of wild grasses. But instead of laying eggs directly onto these foodplants, female Ringlets may simply scatter them indiscriminately among the grasses, even when in flight.

Common Blue

Small and exquisitely coloured, blue butterflies are among our most beautiful insects. The UK is fortunate to have nine resident species, their delicate wings ranging from light powder blue to vibrant azure and, confusingly, brown. Among some species, including the **Common Blue**, the male is blue while the female is usually brown.

Given the variations, identifying our blue butterflies is not always easy and it helps to observe both the top wing colour and patterned underside (*right*). Habitat and time of year can also narrow down possibilities.

The Common Blue is the commonest of our blue butterflies and a handsome member of the clan. The males are a conspicuous bright blue, their outlines fringed with white, and their undersides have orange marks near the edges of the wings, which help distinguish them from the **Holly Blue** (*see box below*).

The female Common Blue is largely brown, with a variable bluish tinge near the body and similar markings on the underside of the wings to males.

Common Blues are widespread and found throughout summer and into autumn across a range of habitats.

Most of our blue butterfly species are scarce and often localised in distribution, among them the rare **Large Blue**, which has been successfully reintroduced after its UK extinction.

Holly Blue

Of the various blue butterflies in Britain, this is the one most likely to be seen flitting around parks and gardens – and is also the first of the year to emerge. If you spot a blue butterfly in April then it will almost certainly be a Holly Blue.

Numbers fluctuate, but in good years there are plenty about from spring until autumn and they are widespread in a variety of habitats.

The Holly Blue's colouring is very similar to that of other blue butterflies. Key to identification are the colour and pattern of the wing undersides, revealed whenever it lands. Its pale blue underwing is subtly marked with little black dots, as if lightly spattered with ink, and lacks the orange of the Common Blue.

As the name suggests it can be found on Holly, where it lays its eggs, and Ivy later in the summer.

Silver-washed Fritillary

The **Silver-washed Fritillary** is the largest of Britain's fritillary butterflies – a rich golden or orangey-brown species which may be seen in high summer in broadleaf woodland glades and along hedgerows, where it feeds on the nectar of Bramble flowers.

Although it has a powerful, gliding flight, the Silver-washed Fritillary can be relatively easy to approach when feeding – and will visit garden flowers.

The species may be recognised by its size – being larger than a **Peacock** butterfly – and the sweeping curve of its front wings.

As with other fritillary species, checking the patterning on the underside of the wings when folded shut helps with identification. Those of the Silver-washed Fritillary are light greenish-brown and, as the name suggests, have washes of silver, like light streaks, running across them. This distinguishes the species from other fritillary butterflies that have light squares or spots, known as 'pearls', on the undersides of their wings.

In some locations a small proportion of Silver-washed Fritillary females lack an orangey hue and have darker spotting on pale upperwings.

The Silver-washed Fritillary was once more widespread, but is now mainly found in the

Dark Green Fritillary

The **Dark Green Fritillary** is a relatively large, fast-flying summer species of flower-rich grasslands – and an attractive member of the fritillary family.

As the name suggests, the Dark Green Fritillary can be identified by its dark green colouring. However this is not on the upperside of its wings, which are golden-orange chequered with black. Instead, when it settles with wings closed, the green hue is visible

The Dark Green Fritillary can be recognised by the greenish wash across its underwings, which are also marked with prominent white spots.

84 BUTTERFLIES

Rare fritillaries

The majority of our fritillary butterflies are rare and threatened species, with colonies often confined to isolated pockets of suitable habitat.

Scarcer species range from the **Marsh**, **Pearl-bordered** and **Small Pearl-bordered** fritillaries to the extremely localised **High Brown**, **Heath** and **Glanville** fritillaries.

The most widespread of these scarcities is the Small Pearl-bordered Fritillary, mainly found in woodland glades in the north and west, while the most distinctive is the Marsh Fritillary (*left*), which has orange, brown and yellow patterning.

Given the restricted distribution of rarer species, finding them requires careful planning so you are in the right habitat and location during the correct flight season and suitable weather conditions.

southern half of Britain, though numbers have been on an upward trend.

The dark patterning on the front wings of male butterflies includes four slightly ridged stripes. These contain so-called 'scent scales' – the pheromones of which are used to attract females. During the dramatic courtship chase, a male showers a flying female with a perfumed confetti of these tiny scales.

The **Gatekeeper** (*see page 81*) also has noticeable patches of scent scales – a dark smudge across each of the male's orange forewings.

Silver-washed Fritillary eggs are laid low down on a shady tree trunk close to wild violets (*right*). The caterpillars that hatch hibernate through winter before eventually descending the tree in spring to feed on the violets.

One common species that could be confused with our fritillary butterflies is the **Comma** (*see page 70*). It has similar golden-orange colouring, marked with dark dots and dashes – however, it can readily be identified by the fact that the edges of its wings are ragged, not smooth.

on the underside, spotted with pearls of white.

This species is the most widespread of our fritillary butterflies, being found from July to August in suitable grassland, downland, heathland, scrub and coastal habitats scattered across Britain. The butterflies are active on sunny days and when feeding are generally attracted to purple flowers, such as thistles.

Telling lookalike fritillary butterflies apart is not easy, given they all have similar upperwings. However, the undersides – often intricately coloured like stained glass windows – provide vital clues when it comes to identification.

When trying to observe a resting or feeding individual it helps to move slowly and steadily, avoiding sudden movements or casting one's shadow over the butterfly. Binoculars offer close-up views and taking photographs with a zoom lens enables subtle distinguishing patterning to be examined.

Small Copper

The **Small Copper** is a fast-flying little dynamo of a butterfly, and when it settles to soak up the sun it stops you in your tracks with its glorious bright copper colouring. Spread wings reveal deep orange marked with dark square spots and darker hindwings.

Good sightings are something to savour as it is an active species. However, the Small Copper will frequently bask in clear view, absorbing the warmth of the sunshine as it takes a break from patrolling territorial air space or feeding.

Small Coppers are relatively common and found across Britain in varied habitats throughout the warmer months.

Britain has a variety of small butterflies. They include the hairstreaks and skippers, which may be spotted on summer walks in woodlands and grasslands. Some of these petite gems can be surprisingly easy to overlook – and challenging to identify. Looking at the undersides when the wings are folded often provides crucial clues to telling them apart.

A number of our smaller butterflies may even be mistaken for moths, given they appear far removed from large and ornate favourites like **Red Admirals** and **Peacocks**.

Fortunately, despite its size, the eye-catching Small Copper is big on looks and character – and of our littlest butterflies it is the one most likely to visit gardens.

In good years this species can squeeze in three generations. The Small Copper passes the winter at the caterpillar stage of its life cycle and pupates as a chrysalis in spring. The butterflies that emerge in April and May breed and lay

Green Hairstreak

While butterflies often have beautifully coloured upperwings, with undersides that are plain by comparison, the **Green Hairstreak** (*left*) is quite the opposite.

The species has brown upperwings, but you seldom see these as it only settles with its wings closed. However, the underside is dazzling. When this delicate little butterfly lands it becomes a precious sliver of gleaming metallic green.

We have five kinds of hairstreak butterfly, and the majority of the species are scarce or elusive. The Green Hairstreak is the most widespread. It is on the wing in May and June and favours warm, sheltered sites across a range of habitats, including heathland, moorland and grassland with patches of scrub – offering close-up views as it perches in sunshine on foliage, such as hawthorn or gorse bushes.

The related **Purple Hairstreak** (*right*) is more common, but

their eggs on sorrel plants. Their offspring eventually develop into flying adults by late summer and these in turn give rise to the next wave of butterflies in early autumn.

Britain was once home to an attractive close relative – the **Large Copper**. This bigger and brighter species of marshy habitats became extinct here by the 1850s, due to the drainage of its fenland haunts. Attempts to reintroduce it from populations on the Continent have so far failed. Other butterflies that have become extinct as resident breeding species in the British Isles include the **Black-veined White** and **Mazarine Blue**.

Large Skipper

Skippers are fast, small butterflies with wingspans of less than 4cm and may be mistaken for moths.

The widespread **Large Skipper** has a stout furry body and faintly chequered golden-brown wings. When at rest, it holds its wings in a most unusual way, with the forewings held up in a 'V' shape.

It is found in areas with long grasses during the summer – as is the common **Small Skipper**, which lacks markings on its plain golden-orange wings.

Three of our skipper species are brown, with light chequered patterning – the most widespread having a rather unflattering name, the **Dingy Skipper** (see pages 69 and 93).

eeps out of view high up amid he canopy of oak trees, the aves of which are eaten by its aterpillars. However, adults will y down to lower vegetation on unny afternoons where they can e more easily observed – the dark pperside having an attractive urple sheen (more extensive in ales than females).

The closed wings are silvery-grey d have a noticeable white line nning across – the light streak, in as a hair, that gives hairstreaks eir name.

Moths

Emperor Moth

The **Emperor Moth** is one of Britain's most spectacular insects, Not only is it large, but its wings are ornately patterned and emblazoned with four dramatic eye-spots.

This is a widespread day-flying species of moth, which can be seen from late March to May fluttering low and purposefully over moorland heather, heaths and dunes. It might easily be mistaken at first glance for a butterfly, being similar in size to a **Small Tortoiseshell** (*see page* **66**).

Emperor Moths spotted flying around by day are males searching for females. The males are attracted to pheromones emitted by the larger and less active females. They pick up the chemical cues using their feathery antennae and are so finely attuned to the wind-blown scent that they can detect it from 1.5km or more away – a staggering distance.

With a wingspan of around 8cm, the stout-bodied nocturnal female is one of our largest resident insects. Both sexes are striking-looking: males (*above*) are patterned with washes of orange, chocolate-brown and strawberry pink, while the shyer females (*right*) have grey markings.

Their prominent eye-spots help foil predators – looming

Variety of moths

White Plume Moth

Moths have earned a reputation as being small, brown and dull. But many of the hundreds of species that live in Britain are quite the opposite. In fact, when it comes to bright colouring, a number would give butterflies a run for their money. They include the tiger moths, burnet moths and elephant hawk-moths featured on these pages, among others. A number also have hindwings that, when spread open, are dazzlingly patterned.

There are roughly 2,500 moth species in Britain – plenty to keep even the most devoted Lepidoptera enthusiast busy, especially when you consider that our resident butterfly species tally is just under 60.

Many people think of moths as clothes-eaters. In fact, there are only a couple of species that cause problems in the home, as their larvae eat natural fibres like wool.

The smaller species are often grouped together under the term

Biggest and smallest

The Emperor Moth is one of Britain's largest moth species. The wingspan of the females is around a palm-width across, and the body is particularly stocky. The **Privet Hawk-moth** (see page 96) has narrower and more pointed wings, but they are even wider, stretching up to 12cm – making it our largest resident moth.

The **Death's-head Hawk-moth** (see page 97) is a rare visitor to the British Isles and slightly bigger still. This powerful flyer has broad tapering wings and a thick body.

At the opposite end of the scale, the UK's smallest moth, the **Pygmy Sorrel Moth** (left), has a wingspan of only 3mm and is one of the world's tiniest moths.

large they may frighten off potential attackers, or fool birds into pecking at the 'eyes', damaging the wing-tip but providing a chance for the moth to escape with its body unharmed.

While the adults only fly in spring, the large caterpillars found in summer are also stunning, commonly feeding on heather. They are bright green, ringed with black stripes that are embellished with bristly orangey-yellow spots (left).

The caterpillar pupates during winter in a papery cocoon, which has the brown fibrous appearance of a tiny coconut and is roughly the same size as a peach stone. Come spring, the moth emerges intent on breeding. It won't feed during its short life on the wing, sustained instead by the weight gained during the caterpillar stage of its life cycle.

The Emperor Moth is related to some of the biggest moths in the world, the giant silk moths. They include the Atlas Moth and the Hercules Moth, both of which have wingspans the width of a dinner plate.

'micro-moths', as distinct from the larger so-called 'macro-moths', of which we have around 900 different kinds. Some of our heftier species, including hawk-moths, are an impressive size, with robust bodies and broad wings.

The moths featured in this book are distinctive, common and widespread, acting as a useful introduction to these fascinating and underappreciated insects.

True Lover's Knot (left) and Canary-shouldered Thorn (right).

Garden Tiger

The **Garden Tiger** is one of our most striking moths, with white and chocolate-brown front wings coupled with vivid orangey-red hindwings – which it flashes when threatened to scare off potential predators.

Numbers of this handsome species, which is on the wing in late summer, have declined since the 1980s, but it is still fairly common and widespread, and can be found in gardens, meadows, open woods and on rough ground.

While the adult is a mottled and striped 'tiger', the caterpillar is known as a 'bear' – the 'woolly bear' (*right*). It is so called as it is particularly furry, with long hairs that are irritating to the touch and make it unappetising to most birds.

The caterpillars, which grow to several centimetres in length, feed on a range of vegetation, including nettles and dock leaves. They use toxic compounds in the plants as part of their own defence mechanisms. Being foul tasting and densely covered with irritating hairs, they successfully avoid being on the menu for most predators. However, perhaps surprisingly, one particular bird is partial to these unusual larvae: the Cuckoo.

The colourful patterning of the adult moth warns that it is also unpalatable. And if a potential predator gets too close, the moths make a rasping sound by rubbing their wings together.

These furry-bodied moths are adapted for a cool climate, but it is believed that warming temperatures could be impacting their numbers – with milder and wetter winters reducing the survival rates of the caterpillars.

The Garden Tiger moth has several close relatives that are equally colourful, though not

Moths versus butterflies

Differences between moths and butterflies are far from clear cut, given they have so many features in common as members of the same taxonomical order of insects: Lepidoptera.

You might imagine that the easiest way to distinguish moths from butterflies is that the former are nocturnal and the latter active by day. However, there are more day-flying moths in the British Isles than all of our butterfly species put together. And butterflies such as the **Red Admiral** will even fly at night on migration.

It is also an oversimplification to consider moths as universally brown and dull in appearance – as the colourful species featured in these pages illustrate.

When not soaking up the warmth of the sun, butterflies close their wings vertically above the body at rest. A number of moth species do likewise, but for the most part moths settle with wings spread horizontally or folded the body in a tent-like fashion.

as widespread, being largely confined to the southern half of Britain.

The **Scarlet Tiger** (*right, top*) has vivid red hindwings, as does the **Jersey Tiger**, which is marked with black bands resembling a series of 'V' shapes. The glorious **Cream-spot Tiger** (*right, below*) sports golden rear wings and a red abdomen. The **Wood Tiger** is localised but widely distributed, and has dark patterning and yellowish hindwings, while the **Ruby Tiger**, with red hindwings, is common, though less ornate than the other tiger moths.

Warning colours

It is no use being toxic or foul-tasting in order to avoid being eaten, unless you advertise that this is the case. Which is why some unpalatable insects, such as tiger moths, are so brightly coloured – predators are quick to associate a vivid appearance with a bitter-tasting mouthful, and learn to avoid the insect in future.

Common warning colours include red and yellow, with contrasting black or white markings. The caterpillars of the **Cinnabar** moth (*see page 100*) are particularly conspicuous (*below*). Their yellow-and-black stripes indicate that they are poisonous, having accumulated toxins from the ragwort they feed on.

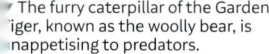

The furry caterpillar of the Garden Tiger, known as the woolly bear, is unappetising to predators.

The most reliable visible distinction is the shape of the antennae. Butterflies typically have club-shaped tips – never the feathery or comb-like structures characteristic of moths. There are exceptions (the antennae of burnet moths look similar to those of butterflies), but as a general rule of thumb the shape of antennae is a significant distinguishing factor.

The Dingy Skipper butterfly (*right*) looks similar to a moth, while the July Thorn moth (*left*) holds its wings vertically at rest, much like a butterfly.

MOTHS 93

Elephant Hawk-moth

This pink-patterned moth is a stunning insect – and fortunately widespread and common enough that you are quite likely to encounter it.

The **Elephant Hawk-moth** is on the wing during the warmer months. Readily attracted to light, it can be encountered flying at an illuminated window or around an outside lamp. Individuals may also be spotted hovering as they feed on the nectar of honeysuckle after dark – their excellent colour-sensitive night vision enabling them to accurately locate flowers.

The name of this gaudy pink-and-greenish-gold moth seems at odds with its appearance, but is actually based on the shape and colour of its mature caterpillar. The large grey-brown larva (green when young) has a tapering body and resembles an elephant's trunk. It is often encountered by gardeners in late summer and autumn as it wanders in search of a place to pupate.

The caterpillar, which feeds on willowherbs and bedstraws, also has large 'eye' marking near the head end. When threatened it rears up with the eye-spots prominent and it is believed this alarming posture is designed to frighten off potential predators by mimicking a snake.

The Elephant Hawk-moth has a lookalike relative called the **Small Elephant Hawk-moth**. Less common, it has more yellowy-gold patterning and lacks the pink stripe running down the abdomen.

Moths and light

Exactly why moths are drawn to light remains something of a mystery. An established theory has it that these nocturnal insects confuse an illuminated bulb with the moon, which they use to navigate. While they can keep the moon in the same position relative to their flight path, they are forced to adjust their direction continually to do the same when they pass a light, flying in ever-decreasing circles.

More recent research suggests that the contrast between a slightly lighter sky and darker ground at night helps moths keep the right way up when flying. Disorientated by artificial light, they tilt their back to the source of the illumination, trying to keep it 'overhead', and end up spiralling in chaotic loops around it.

Moth traps exploit the behaviour and consist of a bulb that produces UV light – particularly attractive to moths – fitted to a container into which the moths fall and may be examined before being released unharmed.

Hummingbird Hawk-moth

This moth is aptly named, resembling a tiny hummingbird as it hovers to feed on the nectar of flowers. Every year, conservation organisations such as the RSPB are contacted by people believing they have seen an actual hummingbird. These birds are not found in Britain, being native to the Americas, but the confusion is understandable, given the behaviour of the day-flying moth.

When hovering the moth's whirring wings are a blur, moving at high speed to keep the insect steady in the air. This enables it to feed with precision from flowers, using its proboscis like a long straw to suck up nectar. Individuals may visit the same flower beds on a daily basis, and the long proboscis is curled up when not in use.

The rapid flight is energy intensive and **Hummingbird Hawk-moths** feed often, attracted to nectar-rich blooms such as honeysuckles, valerians and verbenas.

The moth has a wingspan of around 5–6cm and is active in sunny weather. It is grey-brown in appearance, but in flight reveals orange in the wings and eye-catching black-and-white chequering at the tail end of the abdomen.

While widespread, the species is most common in the south, and may be spotted in parks, gardens and the wider countryside.

Not quite a Hummingbird Hawk-moth?

Although Hummingbird Hawk-moths breed in the British Isles, they are not generally able to survive our winters and so our population is predominantly the result of migration from the south, with varying numbers arriving from the Continent every year.

During the warmer months another migrant day-flying moth is commonly seen feeding at flowers in parks, gardens and grassland habitats. This species is the **Silver Y** moth – so named because of the pale mark on the grey-brown front wings resembling the letter 'Y'.

The Silver Y has a 3–4cm wingspan. It is active by day and night, wings quivering as it moves from flower to flower. At rest, it holds its wings in a tent-like shape over its body, common to many moths.

Silver Ys can be abundant some years, particularly in southern countries. in Britain they cannot survive our winter frosts, so the population here is the result of fresh influxes every spring and summer from Europe.

MOTHS 95

Poplar Hawk-moth

The hawk-moths are a family of species which include among their number some of the largest of our moths. These heavyweights, with broad wingspans and thick bodies, are impressive and often attractively marked insects – and we are fortunate to have a variety in Britain.

Our larger hawk-moths are active at night, and attracted to light, so may enter lit buildings after dark or be encountered around outside lamps or illuminated windows.

The common **Poplar Hawk-moth** is sometimes chanced across by day, resting on a tree trunk or a wall near to an outside light that had drawn it during the night. Even though it is brown and grey, and well camouflaged, its size and unusual posture catch the eye.

At rest the hindwings are held in front of the forewings, while the abdomen may be curled upwards. Its body is thick as a cigar and the span of the scalloped-edged wings reaches 9cm.

If disturbed, the moth flashes its wings, revealing a rufous patch on the hindwings designed to startle any potential predator.

Other large hawk-moths

The **Eyed Hawk-moth** (*left*) looks similar to the Poplar Hawk-moth when at rest. However, if threatened it spreads its wings to expose dazzling blue eye-spots on the pinkish-tinged hindwings – an alarming sight for any potential predator. The Eyed Hawk-moth also has a distinctive dark patch behind the head.

The **Privet Hawk-moth** (*near right*), found in June and July across southern Britain, is the largest of our resident moths with a wingspan of up to 12cm. The thorax behind the head is black and the pointed, narrow wings have a light front edge, while the thick abdomen and hindwings are marked with pink-and-black stripes. The large green caterpillar with a curved tail and purple-and-white stripes, is equally impressive.

The **Lime Hawk-moth** (*far right*) is an attractive moth with distinctive ragged-edged wings

Fascinating family

Hawk-moths belong to a taxonomic family known as Sphingidae, of which there are more than 1,000 species worldwide.

Often large, attractively patterned and able to migrate over considerable distances, they have long captivated naturalists and scientists. There is even a museum dedicated solely to Sphingidae in the Czech Republic.

Hawk-moths are among the most-studied insect groups, and their size means it is possible for individuals to be tracked on migration using a small transmitter attached to the body.

Best known of the species is the **Death's-head Hawk-moth** (*below*), which has featured in novels, paintings and films, famously appearing on the poster for the chilling movie *The Silence of the Lambs*. It bears a sinister skull-like marking on its thorax.

The Poplar Hawk-moth is a widespread resident species and its caterpillars feed on the leaves of willows, sallows and – as the name suggests – poplar trees.

The stout caterpillars grow to around 8cm in length and are pale green with creamy-yellow diagonal stripes on the sides (*far left*). The end of the caterpillar has a little upward-pointing tail, known as a 'horn'. This is a characteristic of hawk-moth larvae, which are called 'hornworms' in some countries, including the US.

Adult Poplar Hawk-moths do not eat, but rely instead on energy reserves built up during the caterpillar stage of their life cycle to sustain them as they fly in search of mates.

They are commonly caught in moth traps, which use a UV light to attract moths at night that can be released unharmed. Female Poplar Hawk-moths tend to be caught during the first few hours of darkness, while males predominantly come to light after midnight.

Moth-trapping sessions run by local natural history groups provide a chance to learn about the impressive diversity of these nocturnal insects.

and greenish banding. The species is reasonably common across southern Britain, including in urban areas such as London where there are plenty of lime trees.

The **Pine Hawk-moth** is grey with dark streaking and its caterpillars eat pine needles.

Visiting migrants from southern climes include the large **Convolvulus Hawk-moth** – resembling a mottled version of the Privet Hawk-moth – and the rare and robust **Death's-head Hawk-moth** (*top*).

MOTHS 97

Drinker

While a wide variety of moths are brown, this hefty species stands out from the crowd on account of its size, thick furry body and distinctive pose at rest.

A widespread species of marshy meadows, moors, grassland and open woodland, the **Drinker** is on the wing in late summer, and attracted to light.

It has golden or orangey-brown wings with an outstretched span of up to 7cm. The wings each have two light dots side by side in the middle and a long, dark line running diagonally across from the inner edge to the tip.

The wings are held upright around the body at rest, the edges pressed tight together like a closed mussel shell. Close-up views reveal a characterful furry face with a pointed snout and the darker males have large, feathered antennae.

The Drinker's name derives from its caterpillar's supposed habit of drinking dew drops. The hairy

Close relatives

The Drinker is a member of a family of similar robust and mainly brown moths called the eggars.

They include among their number the **Oak Eggar** (*left*) – a common summer species with sandy or brown wings that have a light band running across them and are marked with a prominent white spot. Those in northern Britain are slightly larger and darker and known as the **Northern Eggar**.

The **Fox Moth** (*right*) is a grassland and heathland species, on the wing in late spring and early summer. The females are

...5cm-long caterpillar is commonly encountered ...n suitable damp grassy habitats and has golden ...speckling on the back and white tufts running ...long the sides.

The eggs are laid in July and August on a variety ...of grasses and reeds, and the caterpillars that ...emerge split their development between one year ...nd the next. They feed and grow in the autumn ...ntil winter sets in, then hibernate through the ...old months. Once temperatures rise, they become ...ctive again and continue feeding again in spring. ...inally, when summer comes around, they pupate ...nd emerge as adults – the females slightly larger ...nd lighter-coloured than the males.

As with butterflies, the annual life cycles of our ...oths – from egg to caterpillar (larva) to pupa to ...dult (imago) – means that they are only on the ...ing for certain periods of the year. The timings ...ary and some have particularly long flight seasons ...uring which they breed, while others are short-...ved. Their life stages also need to be synchronised ...ith those of the foodplants upon which their ...aterpillars depend.

Chemical cues

The large feathery antennae of male Drinker moths are designed to pick up the wind-blown chemical scents (pheromones) of females – and find them in the dark!

Research into moth pheromones has enabled synthetic versions to be manufactured which can be used to attract target species. These lures, replicating the chemical scents of females, may be deployed to survey moths that are not attracted to light and difficult to locate by traditional means – such as day-flying clearwing moths.

Commercially available lures (*below*) are also used to trap so-called 'pest' species, such as the non-native **Box-tree Moth**, the caterpillars of which damage the foliage of Box hedges.

Adult Drinker moths can only be seen in high summer – so you won't spot one fluttering about in April or May. However, the related December Moth (*see below*) flies between October and December.

...ey-brown and the males reddish-...own. The rounded forewings of ...oth sexes are marked with two ...ght lines and lack any white spot. ... with the Oak Eggar, males are ...tive in the day, flying in search ... females on sunny afternoons. ...e Fox Moth caterpillar is dark ...d orangey-brown on top with ...aggy hairs.

The **December Moth** (*right*) is ...dark grey-brown species which, ...the name suggests, is on the ...ng in winter, when very few other ...oths are out and about. The

December Moth's charcoal wings are marked with light wavy lines and the furry head is light in colour. It is attracted to outside lights and illuminated windows.

Large feathery antennae enable male December Moths (*above*) to detect the wind-blown pheromones of females.

Six-spot Burnet

The **Six-spot Burnet** is a conspicuous moth, with red-and-black wings and long, thick antennae.

It is active by day and perfectly at home out in the open, in full view of potential predators such as birds. However, the Six-spot Burnet has little to fear, given it is not only unpalatable but also potentially toxic, producing the chemical compound hydrogen cyanide.

There are a number of different burnet moths, but the Six-spot is the most common and widespread. The hindwings are red with a black border, while the dark forewings have a lustrous sheen and each is marked like a dice with six red spots – as opposed to the five wing-spots of some other burnet moth species.

Burnet moths are found in grassy places, such as downland and coastal meadows, and are weak flyers, fluttering fairly low to the ground on hot summer days and often settling on thistles and knapweed to feed.

They may be confused with the **Cinnabar** moth (*below*), which has similar colouration and red spots, but the Cinnabar also has a thin line of red along the front edge of the forewing.

Occasionally, Six-spot Burnets are found with yellow instead of red spots.

Cinnabar

Much like the Six-spot Burnet, the Cinnabar moth is a species typically encountered during the summer in grassy open areas, such as coastal fields, rabbit-grazed pasture, on rough ground or among sand dunes.

Cinnabar moths are easily disturbed by day – their stunning scarlet hindwings, visible in flight, stopping you in your tracks in amazement as they flutter off from low vegetation.

Once they settle you can admire their smart appearance, though they tend to tuck their bright hindwings out of view at rest. Each dark front wing is marked with a dash and two dots – a red line running down the outer edge and two red spots at the broad wing-tip.

The caterpillars of this common and widespread species are particularly distinctive, banded with yellow and black, and can be spotted feeding on ragwort. Their colouring warns birds that they are poisonous (*see page 93*).

Peppered Moth

The **Peppered Moth** is a species that may ring a bell among those who studied science at school as it provides a fascinating example of Darwin's evolution by natural selection in action.

The moth is generally white, peppered with black speckles on the wings, and well camouflaged when resting by day on the lichen-covered branches and trunks of trees.

A naturally occurring genetic mutation causes some to have black wings (*below*), but this means they are more easily spotted in rural settings by birds and eaten before they have a chance to breed.

However, in the nineteenth century, industrial and domestic coal fires resulted in walls and trees in urban areas becoming blackened with soot, which led to lichen dying off. Here the dark (melanic) form of Peppered Moth blended in better than the typical lighter version – and by avoiding predation these sooty-black moths rapidly became the dominant type found in cities. A case of 'survival of the fittest' – that is, survival of the best adapted to environmental conditions and the challenges of life.

Pollution controls in the twentieth century led to improved air quality, resulting in the return of lichen in built-up areas – and the standard pale Peppered Moth became the commonest kind once again.

This species is common across Britain and can be found from May to August in gardens and parks as well as the wider countryside. Thick-bodied and fairly large, the Peppered Moth rests with wings spread wide and is well camouflaged. The caterpillars, which feed on the leaves of a variety of trees and shrubs, resemble a twig to avoid being spotted by birds.

Not quite a Peppered Moth?

If it is spring and your 'Peppered Moth' has brown bands across its wings, then it could be an **Oak Beauty**.

This attractive and common woodland moth is out and about early in the year, being found between February and April. It has white and black-speckled wings, similar to a Peppered Moth, but marked with dark-edged wavy chestnut bands.

Males have feather-like antennae, used to detect wind-blown female pheromones. Like the Peppered Moth, the Oak Beauty may be attracted to light.

Buff-tip

Moths have plenty of predators and are particularly at risk of being eaten when resting and visible during daylight hours. As a result, many species are brown, grey or green in colour to blend in with their surroundings.

A number go a step further and have evolved remarkable shapes and patterns to help avoid detection or to deter hungry birds.

Given their ability to hide within plain sight, these masters of camouflage and disguise are seldom encountered by day. However, they may be attracted to light at night where their beauty and ingenuity can be admired close-up.

Among them is the **Buff-tip** moth – an absolute marvel when it comes to concealment, being not only the same colour as a twig, but the same shape too.

It holds its wings at rest close to the body so that it takes on a stick-like appearance. The mottled silvery-grey colour is similar to that of the bark of trees such as birch, on which caterpillars feed, while pale yellow-brown areas at either end resemble exposed wood, as if a broken fragment.

A medium-sized species, the Buff-tip is common in parks and gardens, flying from May to July, and is attracted to lights late at night.

The **Angle Shades** (*right*) is another well-camouflaged species. With its raggedy-edged wings and autumnal colours, this medium-sized moth looks just like a dead or withered leaf. It is a cunning disguise, and the angular patterning helps break up its outline and adds to the illusion.

A common and widely distributed species, frequently found in gardens, the Angle Shades

Masters of camouflage

The **Merveille du Jour** (*below*) is one of our most beautiful moths, with light peppermint-green wings flecked with black and white.

At rest it blends in perfectly with lichen-mottled bark, and its exquisite colouring gave rise to its French name, which translates marvel – or wonder – of the day.

It is on the wing in the autumn, and frequents woodlands and parks, where its caterpillars feed on oak buds and leaves.

Another well-camouflaged species is the **Green Carpet** moth (*right*). Despite its name, this moth is not an indoor pest with an appetite for floor coverings, but an outdoor species with markings a bit like an intricately woven mat.

There are several related 'carpet' species, such as the **Garden**

Off-putting looks

One way of deterring potential predators is to send out a clear message that you are not good to eat. Some moths deploy bright colours to advertise the fact that they are unsavoury or toxic.

The small grubby-white **Chinese Character** (*below*) takes a unique approach, using visual mimicry to let it be known it is best avoided: it resembles a bird dropping!

The harmless **Lunar Hornet Moth** (*above*) is even more impressive, looking very similar to a hornet. It is a member of a family of moths that have clear wings and bands across the body, closely resembling flies, wasps and hornets.

will come to a light at night. Individuals resting in a prominent spot, such as on a fence post, may also be spotted during the day by the keen-eyed observer.

The Angle Shades moth is a strong flier and the population in areas of Britain is supplemented in late summer by individuals arriving from mainland Europe.

Moths also need to deploy the art of keeping a low profile at other stages in their life cycle, and many caterpillars resemble twigs or have the same colouring as the leaves they eat.

◀ Angle Shades

arpet, **Common Carpet**, **ommon Marbled Carpet** d **Flame Carpet**. All are fairly nilar in appearance, being small d dainty, their wings typically orned with wavy bands and ottled patterning that acts as ective camouflage.

The **Large Emerald** (*right*) is a licate butterfly-like moth with nt green wings that make it hard predators to spot among the sh leaves of trees. As the name ggests, this common summer ecies is relatively large, with a ngspan of 5–6cm.

MOTHS 103

Large Yellow Underwing

There are various moths with 'underwing' in the name that are a fairly plain brown or grey when settled with wings folded, but are characterised by bright and eye-catching hindwings.

These hindwings may be tucked away at rest and become fully visible when they fly, ranging in colour from crimson to deep orange and yellow, depending on the species.

The **Large Yellow Underwing** is an abundant stout-bodied and strong-flying moth which is found across Britain in summer and autumn. It is readily attracted to light and may also be disturbed by day in vegetation – sometimes scuttling away in a mouse-like fashion.

The narrow upperwings are well camouflaged, being a mottled reddish-brown in males and paler grey-brown among females. The underwings are golden yellow with a narrow black band at the outer edge, and this flash of colour may confuse or deter predators like birds.

Underwing moths are not always easy to identify given the similarities between species. The assorted names illustrate the potential for confusion. Alongside the Large Yellow Underwing there is the **Lesser Yellow Underwing**, the **Least Yellow Underwing**, the **Broad-bordered Yellow**

Sugaring

At night, the best way to attract many species of moth is by using a light, such as a moth trap fitted with a UV bulb which catches species unharmed for recording before being released.

But for those who don't have a moth trap, there is another technique which can be worth a try – if you don't mind a little simple cookery...

Called 'sugaring', it involves mimicking the nectar and sap that provides fuel for those moths that have a 'sweet tooth' (not that they have teeth – rather a thin tube-like proboscis for sucking up nutrients).

Sugaring involves painting a rich, syrupy solution onto tree trunks and regularly visiting by torchlight during the night to see what has turned up to feed.

Recipes and measurements vary, but typically involve gently heating around 500ml of brown ale in a pan, then stirring in 1kg of dark brown sugar until it dissolve before adding a tin of black treac A tot of rum near the end may al boost its potency!

Imaginative names

The assorted and intriguing names of our moths add to their appeal and the pleasure of identification. Inventive and idiosyncratic, they are inspired by plants, places, markings and the whims of the Victorian naturalists who named them.

Some reflect the upper-class lifestyles of entomologists of the time, such as the ermines, brocades and footmen. Others illustrate the vivid imaginations of collectors, including species like the **True Lover's Knot**, **Powdered Quaker** and **Maiden's Blush** (*left*).

Lepidopterists of the past also seemingly had a sense of humour when christening less distinctive species, with moth names including the **Uncertain**, the **Anomalous**, the **Suspected** and the **Confused**.

Underwing, the **Lesser Broad-bordered Yellow Underwing**...

That's just for starters, with the **Copper Underwing**, **Orange Underwing** and **Dark Crimson Underwing** adding to the colour mix.

The Broad-bordered Yellow Underwing is a common and widespread species which resembles the Large Yellow Underwing, but has a thicker black band around the edge of the yellow hindwing, as the name suggests.

One particularly handsome variety, the **Red Underwing** (*right*), has crimson hindwings marked with black. Common in late summer and autumn across central and southern Britain, and gradually spreading north, this large species can be attracted with 'sugaring' techniques (*see below*).

Arguably the UK's most spectacular underwing moth is the very rare **Blue Underwing**, long considered the Holy Grail of finds among naturalists. It is more properly known as the Clifden Nonpareil – after the place where it was first recorded and the fact that it was considered beyond compare, from the French 'without equal'. Spreading its mottled upperwings, which span more than 9cm, it reveals inky-black hindwings crossed with a bar of light blue.

This sticky mixture is then painted in lines at eye-height onto tree trunks at dusk. Warm, humid nights with little wind are generally best.

A Large Yellow Underwing moth uses its thin proboscis to suck up sugar solution painted onto a tree trunk.

White Ermine

A number of our moths have a refined beauty, understated colouring and intricate patterning which sets them apart. Some also have wonderfully descriptive names that add to their allure.

The **White Ermine** is perfectly named – its white wings freckled with black spots resembling the ermine fur robes worn by nobility and royalty down the ages.

This smart and attractive moth, with a wingspan of around 4.5cm, can be found in urban gardens and rural areas. Some are spottier than others, with occasional individuals having scarcely any black speckling at all.

If it feels in danger, such as when handled, the White Ermine may play dead, remaining motionless for a short while, even on its back, before coming back to life and scuttling off or flying away.

A closely related species called the **Buff Ermine** is, as the name suggests, off-white. The dark dots on its beige wings are more orderly than those of the White Ermine, forming a diagonal row.

There is also an unrelated group of little species known as small ermine moths (*the* **Bird-cherry Ermine** *is shown below left*). They look like tiny, slender versions of the White Ermine. However, their caterpillars do things on a large scale, creating extensive communal webs that can festoon hedgerows and trees.

Witches and works of art

One day-flying moth of meadow habitats has somewhat sinister markings (*right*). The light patterning on each of the front wings is said to resemble the outline of an old crone's face, which has given rise to its name: **Mother Shipton**, after a sixteenth-century Yorkshire woman who was reputed to be a witch.

Far cheerier is the **Peach Blossom**, its wings decorated as if with floral patterning. The blotches of pale pink on a brown background break up its outline and help provide camouflage.

The delightful **Frosted Orange** is marbled with swirls of golden-orange and is common in a range of habitats, including gardens, while the equally well-named **Burnished Brass** has a greenish-gold lustre that resembles polished metal.

The **Buff Arches** moth is exquisitely patterned in caramel and cream. Its grey wings are marked with brushstrokes of warm brown and delicate ripples of white. A natural work of art in miniature.

Magpie

A black-and-white patterning gives the **Magpie** moth its name, but it also has orangey-gold areas in the wings which make it quite distinctive – and its bold colours warn predators that it is distasteful. Its caterpillars have the same colours and markings as the adults.

Widespread and fairly common, the Magpie can be found during summer in gardens, woodlands and parks, and may be stumbled across by day or found coming to light at night.

There is a similar moth called the **Small Magpie**, but this species lacks the yellow-orange colouring in the wings.

A common species related to the Magpie is the **Brimstone Moth** – and it also stands out on account of its bright appearance (*left*).

This medium-sized yellow moth may be readily identified by its colouring, and the chestnut-brown blotches on the leading edge of its wings. Brimstones can be spotted throughout the warmer months fluttering about at dusk in a range of habitats including gardens, and are also drawn to light at night.

While the adult is eye-catching, the Brimstone caterpillar is a master of camouflage, closely resembling a twig when at rest.

Both the Brimstone and Magpie moths are members of the family Geometridae (*see below*).

Butterfly-like moths

A wide variety of moths have a delicate appearance and fluttering flight which resembles that of a butterfly. They can rest with their broad wings spread out flat and have slender bodies and pretty patterning.

Many such species are members of the large and diverse family of moths known as Geometridae. This scientific term, derived from Ancient Greek, translates as 'world measurer' and refers to the various species' caterpillars – sometimes called 'inch-worms' or 'loopers' for their specific style of movement. Instead of crawling along, these larvae bend in a loop as they move in extended strides, the front end reaching forward and back end catching up, as if measuring out the world inch by inch.

Geometridae species include the **Swallow-tailed Moth** (*left*), a large butterfly-like moth of late summer, measuring 5cm across. This widespread nocturnal species is a smart pale yellow, marked with diagonal lines, and has even been described as resembling a 'flying Post-it note'!

Caterpillar defences

The caterpillars of many moths are small and green or brown, but a few stand out from the crowd with their eccentric appearance. Some are well camouflaged to blend in with their surroundings or brightly coloured to advertise they are distasteful, while others are masters of disguise, covered with irritating hairs, or have an appearance designed to alarm potential predators.

Pale Tussock ▼

Few caterpillars look quite as alien as this 4.5cm green-and-yellow hairy larva, which bears four pale tufts resembling shaving brushes on its back, along with a thin red tuft at the rear. They can be seen between May and October, feeding on a wide range of plants, and are fairly common and widespread. In the autumn they crawl about looking for somewhere suitable to pupate – but don't handle them as the hairs may cause a skin irritation. The adult grey moths rest with their furry legs stretched out in front in a distinctive fashion – a trait shared with the adult Puss Moth.

Vapourer ▲

This odd-looking 4cm critter shares the dorsal 'shaving brushes' of the Pale Tussock caterpillar, and also sports hairy horns – not exactly edible-looking to a passing predator. It can be found on a variety of deciduous trees or shrubs in woodland, parks and gardens from May to September, and is common in many urban areas.

▼ The Pale Tussock is a fairly plain grey moth that stretches its furry front legs forwards at rest (*inset*). Its bristly green-and-yellow caterpillar is much more striking, looking far from appetising for any potential predator.

Puss Moth

The caterpillar of this furry black-and-white moth is certainly a strange beast, with its large pinkish face and thin whip-like tails. When disturbed it rears up, swishing its tails in a display likely to deter a curious bird. If that doesn't work, it will even squirt formic acid at an attacker. They can be seen from June to September in parks, gardens and wetlands, feeding on the leaves of willows and poplars.

Sycamore

Yellow with tufts of orange hair and white diamonds along the back, the eye-catching caterpillar of this moth feeds on sycamore,

maple and other trees including Horse Chestnut from June to September. One of our hairiest and brightest caterpillars, this 4cm-long larva may be chanced across in south-eastern woodlands, gardens, parks and scrub in late summer searching for somewhere to pupate.

Lackey

This caterpillar throws blue into the colour mix with a stripe along the side and a blue head, along with dark eye-spots that give it a rather endearing expression. Lackey caterpillars can be seen on Hawthorn and Blackthorn, among other foodplants, from April to June – mainly in southern Britain – and live communally in silky webs while they feed, growing to 4.5cm in length.

Lobster Moth

This moth of southern Britain is named after its freakish caterpillar, which looks more like a crustacean than an insect larva. If alarmed, the reddish-brown 7cm caterpillar arches its abdomen over its back and splays its legs in a menacing fashion. It can be seen from June to September, mainly feeding on beech, but also oak, birch and hazel.

MOTHS 109

Dragonflies and damselflies

Emperor Dragonfly

This is our largest resident dragonfly – big, bold and beautiful.

The **Emperor Dragonfly** is also a powerful flier and formidable predator – snatching insects in flight using its spiny legs, despatching catches with sharp mouthparts and even eating small prey on the wing. Insects on the menu for this voracious predator include other dragonflies and even butterflies.

The Emperor inhabits large, well-vegetated ponds, lakes, canals and slow-flowing rivers. Males are highly territorial and will patrol their precious patch of water ceaselessly in fine weather – living up to their name as they rule supreme over their domain, chasing off rival dragonflies.

Both sexes have clear wings, which span more than 10cm, and a green thorax (the front body section behind the head to which wings and legs attach). The male is particularly glorious, sporting a bright blue abdomen (the long tail end), with a black stripe down the middle, while females generally have a green abdomen.

The females lay their eggs in aquatic vegetation at the water's surface. The larvae that hatch grow to become large and fearsome underwater predators, eating any living prey they can grab – ranging from small freshwater invertebrates to tadpoles and even fish fry.

The aquatic larvae (*left*) look vaguely like wingless adults, only

Dragons and damsels

Dragonflies are fascinating, eye-catching and spectacular insects. Often brightly coloured, they can be masterful aerial predators, combining agility with an impressive turn of speed, and bring elegance and drama to any stretch of water.

The various related kinds of Odonata, as their taxonomical grouping is known, can be separated into dragonflies – which are typically robust, powerful fliers that spread their wings at right-angles to the body when at rest (*left*); and damselflies – which are characteristically smaller, more dainty and hold their wings together over their back (*right*).

A total of 46 dragonfly and damselfly species are resident in the UK or regular migrants, although a number are very rare or localised in distribution.

Dragonflies and damselflies are mostly active in warm, sunny

Golden-ringed Dragonfly

This large and stunning dragonfly is relatively easy to identify, being black all over and marked with golden rings. They also have green eyes – though these are brown in immature adults.

Golden-ringed Dragonflies lay their eggs in running water that is slightly acidic, such as peaty streams on moorland and heathland, though may be found hunting far from breeding sites.

The female has a little spike at the tail end called an 'ovipositor', used for laying eggs. At nearly 8.5cm in length, females are the longest dragonflies in Britain.

Golden-ringed Dragonflies are particularly long-lived at the aquatic larva stage of their life cycle, which may last between two to five years.

shorter, plumper and brown in colour. This is by far the longest stage of the dragonfly's life cycle, lasting for one to two years before they are ready to become flying adults.

Unlike butterflies and moths, dragonflies do not have a pupa stage. Instead a mature larva climbs up out of the water, clings to vegetation and moults directly into a winged adult. It breaks out of its larval skin and then waits for its wings to stretch and harden before flying off.

Empty larval cases, known as exuviae, may be spotted attached to waterside reeds – evidence of dragonflies successfully making it through to adulthood.

Emperor Dragonflies are widespread in the summer months and most common in southern Britain, though have been increasing in number and range. Distribution surveys show this resilient species is spreading northwards, seemingly taking advantage of a warming climate.

◀ A female Emperor Dragonfly lays eggs on aquatic vegetation.

weather. Identifying them is easiest when they settle on vegetation, and it can be useful to take a photograph from above and the side, as some species are distinguished by small details in their markings and colour.

Globally, this is a successful group of insects, numbering thousands of species and distant relatives were flying around ponds and rivers well before dinosaurs roamed the Earth. Fossil records show one particularly huge dragonfly-like ancestor had wings spanning three-quarters of a metre. An unnerving sight for any smaller insects of the time!

Common Hawker

This large, fast-flying and attractive dragonfly is on the wing in summer and autumn.

Widespread in mainly northern and western areas of Britain, the **Common Hawker** favours stretches of water for breeding that are faintly acidic, such as lakes and pools on peatland heaths and upland moors.

Males (*above*) have blueish eyes and blue pairs of dots running down the long dark abdomen, while females (*left*) are browner in tone and have paired yellow dots on the abdomen. One key identification feature is the thin yellow border along the front edge of the wings.

Common Hawkers tend to be wary and less easy to observe closely than other bolder species. This active dragonfly always seems to be on the move, flying low over water, high above neighbouring fields and along woodland edges.

Hawker dragonflies are so called because of their hunting technique – 'hawking' to and fro on the wing like avian raptors in search of aerial prey. Unfortunately, they can themselves fall prey

Southern Hawker

Most common across southern Britain, the **Southern Hawker** is a dragonfly of lowland lakes, ditches and canals, as well as garden ponds. It can be a confident and inquisitive species, often hovering close as it gives human visitors to its watery habitat a quick once-over.

Closely resembling the Common Hawker, the Southern Hawker has paired green spots running down the long, dark abdomen. However, unlike the Common Hawker, the tip of the tail end is marked with two solid bands, rather than dots.

The Southern Hawker also lacks a thin yellow leading edge to the wings, which is a distinguishing feature of the Common Hawker. Male Southern Hawkers have pale blue markings along their sides and their tail bands are blue, while females are browner in tone.

Both sexes have prominent thick green dashes on the top of their dark 'shoulders' and blocks of green on the sides of their thorax – just beneath where the wings join the body.

This species has been faring relatively well, increasing in number and range over recent years as it pushes north, with localised populations now established in Scotland. Rising temperatures and the creation of new ponds and wetlands have aided its upward trend.

Brown Hawker

This dragonfly is well named, being mainly brown, apart from a scattering of light blue or yellowish markings along the sides. Even its wings have a golden-brown hue.

A lowland species, the **Brown Hawker** breeds in water bodies such as lakes, flooded gravel pits, marshes and canals. It is more tolerant than many species of water pollution.

This large dragonfly often hunts for insect prey away from water and is on the wing in late summer and early autumn.

The Brown Hawker is common in central and southern Britain, but largely absent from Scotland and the south-west.

to actual raptors. Despite turns of speed and manoeuvrability, hawker dragonflies may be caught mid-air by birds such as the Hobby, an agile falcon that targets dragonflies over wetlands (*below right*).

Female Common Hawkers lay their eggs on aquatic vegetation at the margins of lakes and ponds, but also deposit them in damp moss and mud at the water's edge. Their rustling wings may be heard as they move amid bankside plants.

The eggs hatch the following spring and it can take a couple more years for the growing aquatic larvae to mature, before eventually emerging from the water and moulting into flying adults. In all, the early stages of the dragonfly's life cycle last for at least three years, while that of the colourful winged adults can be measured in weeks.

The Common Hawker is easy to confuse with the very similar, but slightly smaller, **Migrant Hawker**. The latter lacks yellow edging at the front of the wings and is more of a lowland species, active well into autumn and common around lakes and ponds in southern Britain.

In late summer our resident population of Migrant Hawkers is boosted by migrants from the Continent.

The Hobby, an agile falcon, catches dragonflies in flight.

Broad-bodied Chaser

If you have just dug a garden pond, you might be surprised to see this hefty-looking dragonfly move in almost as soon as you wind up the hose and put the shovel back in the shed.

The **Broad-bodied Chaser** is quick to establish new territories at small pools, lakes and ditches, and rewards those who create ponds. These active dragonflies are impressive looking, and animate water bodies in summer with their darting flight.

Males are, as the name suggests, wide in the body – as if flattened out – and a striking powder blue when mature (*above*). They vigilantly patrol their little patch of water against intruders, taking up vantage points on surrounding vegetation. The perfect perch, such as a stick overhanging a pond, is returned to time and again.

Females are even broader than males, but golden in colour (*below*). Both sexes have brown eyes, a short, light stripe on each 'shoulder', yellow flecks along the sides of the abdomen and large dark patches where the clear wings join the body.

The Broad-bodied Chaser inhabits small water bodies across much of England and Wales and its range is gradually spreading north.

Females hover low over the water to deposit their eggs on submerged vegetation.

The aquatic larvae have an even more squat appearance than the parent dragonflies.

Four-spotted Chaser

Dragonflies have a dark or coloured marking near the tip of each wing's front edge. However, the **Four-spotted Chaser** is distinctive in having an additional marking in the middle of the leading edge of each wing. With four spots in total across the front wings and four on the hind pair, it could actually have been named the Eight-spotted Chaser!

Common and widespread,

Scarcer species

The **Keeled Skimmer** (*left*) is a species of heathland pools and moorland bogs, particularly in the west.

Both sexes have a slightly raised black line, or 'keel', running down the centre of the tail (abdomen) and a yellow-orange spot near the tip of each wing. When resting they often hold their wings forward at an angle, rather than horizontal to the body.

The **Scarce Chaser** is found in the southern half of England, with East Anglia its stronghold. Males are light blue and have blue eyes, while the females are amber-coloured with black triangular markings down the abdomen.

It can take between one and three years before they are fully developed and clamber up out of the water to moult into flying adults, with the peak emergence being in May.

A number of dragonflies have similar colouring to the Broad-bodied Chaser, though none are as thickset. They include the **Black-tailed Skimmer**.

The mature male of this species (*below*) has a narrow light blue abdomen, which darkens towards the tip – as the name suggests. The female (*right*) is golden-yellow and has two black stripes running down her tail end which are linked with thin horizontal lines to create a 'ladder' effect.

Most common in central and south-eastern England, the Black-tailed Skimmer has spread across much of England and Wales in recent decades and is gradually pushing north. It inhabits lakes, reservoirs and flooded gravel pits, and often basks in the sun on muddy or sandy shorelines.

The Four-spotted Chaser is an attractive golden-brown species of well-vegetated water bodies. It has a tapering abdomen that is narrower than that of the Broad-bodied Chaser and darkens towards the tip.

In contrast to other chasers and skimmers, male and female Four-spotted Chasers look alike. Males are territorial and dart out from their perch to check out any other dragonflies straying into their patch. Rivals are seen off and females pursued.

After mating, the male may guard the female, protecting her from being harassed while she is laying her eggs. She does this by hovering low over the lake or pond and repeatedly dipping the end of her abdomen into the water – a technique shared with other chaser and skimmer species.

DRAGONFLIES AND DAMSELFLIES

Common Darter

Skimmers, hawkers, chasers, darters... our dragonflies have wonderful names that help to describe their behavioural traits. Darters do indeed live up to their name, darting out from perches to see off territorial rivals, check out potential mates or capture flying prey.

The **Common Darter** is an abundant small dragonfly, around 4cm in length, which inhabits a range of freshwater habitats, from garden ponds to lakes and canals. Males are orangey-red, with clear wings and brown eyes, while females are golden-brown.

Dragonflies are typically on the wing from late spring until early autumn, but the widespread Common Darter survives late into the year and may be active on mild sunny days even in December.

It can be spotted basking on bare earth in sheltered and sunny spots while it warms up, or perched overlooking its watery domain, frequently with wings held slightly forwards. When it does dart off to inspect passing dragonflies or to ambush prey, it often returns to the same lookout position.

Just to confuse matters, there are a couple of

Life cycle

Dragonflies and damselflies have a fascinating life cycle, with most of their lives spent underwater as larvae.

Eggs are laid close to or in water, and the carnivorous larvae that emerge eat live aquatic prey – such as water fleas, leeches and tadpoles – growing steadily over months or even years.

When fully grown, larvae climb out and hatch into winged adults (*left*). These newly emerged dragonflies and damselflies are pale to begin with, but gradually develop their bright colouring. They feed up and mature away from water, before returning to breed.

The males of some species are highly territorial, chasing away rivals. Other species tolerate company and so can be found in abundance, as is the case with a number of damselflies.

Mating sees pairs locked together in a 'wheel'. The male

Black Darter

Our smallest resident dragonfly, the **Black Darter** is no bigger than a pen top, at only 3.5cm in length.

As the name suggests, the male has a mainly black body, as well as black eyes and legs. The female is a golden-brown colour, similar to other female darters, but sports a dark triangle marking just behind the head.

This is a species of bogs, ditches, pools and shallow water on heathland and moorland. Scattered populations are found in suitable habitat across the British Isles, but the Black Darter is most common and widespread in northern and western Britain. However, the species has declined over recent decades.

other scarcer British darters with similar colouring. The most commonly encountered of these lookalikes is the **Ruddy Darter** (*above*), mostly found in the southern half of Britain.

The legs of the Ruddy Darter are jet black, while the dark legs of the Common Darter usually have a thin pale yellowish stripe running down them. Male Ruddy Darters are crimson red and have a slightly swollen tip to the tail end.

Taking photos to examine details of markings can be useful when it comes to identification – and it helps that these close relatives like to sit on favoured perches in the sunshine in full view.

Cameras with a zoom or long lens enable you to get close-up images of dragonflies without disturbing these flighty insects. Using a mobile phone camera requires a stealthy approach. Given dragonflies have excellent eyesight, you should move slowly and steadily and avoid casting a shadow over the subject.

Binoculars are also an essential tool for identifying species – in particular, models with close focus, enabling detailed views of dragonflies perched just a few feet away.

uses claspers at the tail end of his abdomen to grasp a female behind the head, while the female reaches forward with the tip of her abdomen to access sperm that the male had previously transferred to an area beneath the front of his body. With some species, possessive males continue to hold on to the female even while she lays her fertilised eggs.

Banded Demoiselle

There are few more enchanting sights in summer than dancing demoiselles. Fluttering along the edges of streams and rivers, these dainty delights look as if they might have flown in from the tropics, being a dazzling metallic blue or green.

Demoiselles are large damselflies, but unusual in having coloured – rather than clear – wings.

They are almost butterfly-like in flight, flitting with broad, shimmering wingbeats at the water's edge, and also perch on bankside vegetation, offering close-up views of their iridescent colouring.

We have two kinds of demoiselle in Britain, the **Banded Demoiselle** and the **Beautiful Demoiselle**.

The male Banded Demoiselle

is distinguished by the broad, dark band across the wings – this fingerprint-like marking enables the species to be readily identified. Males also draw attention to themselves by flicking their wings open and 'dancing' in the air to catch the eye of passing females.

The wings of female Banded Demoiselles lack the dark band. Instead they are translucent with a greenish tint and have a prominent white spot close to the tip (*left*). Females have a gleaming green body while the body of males is a lustrous blue-green.

They are common in southern Britain, including most of England and Wales, but become rarer moving northwards.

Beautiful Demoiselle

The Beautiful Demoiselle is a fairly common resident of streams and river habitats in mainly southern and western Britain – and may be numerous in some areas beside suitable sandy-bottomed stretches of running water.

The wings are tinted dark brown or black and have an iridescent sheen in the sunlight.

Males have a shiny blue-green body and often perch on bankside vegetation – flitting out on dark wings to catch prey or defend their territory before returning to a favoured perch.

Females have a glossy green body and may be confused with female Banded Demoiselles

– however, the wings of female Beautiful Demoiselles are darker with a brownish, rather than pale greenish, hue.

Large Red Damselfly

Our 20-odd species of damselfly are typically blue or green in colour and can be tricky to tell apart. However, the **Large Red Damselfly** stands out from the crowd, being a striking red colour.

This is an abundant and widespread species found in most freshwater and wetland habitats, including bogs, ditches, canals, lakes and well vegetated garden ponds.

The male Large Red Damselfly (*above*) is a thin stick of crimson, with black legs and a dark patch near the tip of the tail. Despite the name, it is less than 4cm in length. The female (*below*) can vary in appearance but tends to look like a darker version of the male.

Both sexes have reddish eyes. On the thorax – the body section between the head and long abdomen – they have a red or yellow stripe on each 'shoulder'.

Large Red Damselflies are among the first damselflies to emerge in spring and can be seen through until autumn. Males will actively chase away rivals from their patch of water.

The Large Red Damselfly has a rare relative called the **Small Red Damselfly** which, as the name suggests, is slightly smaller. This scarce lookalike is found at scattered sites in southern Britain and identified by its reddish – rather than black – legs.

Emerald Damselfly

The widespread **Emerald Damselfly** has a metallic green body, similar to the larger demoiselles (*see opposite page*), but differs in that its wings are clear and it often holds them half-open at rest, rather than closed above the body. This unusual trait has given rise to an alternative name for the species: Common Spreadwing.

Mature male Emerald Damselflies have blue eyes and pale blue bands at the top and bottom of their long shiny green abdomen. The female has a slightly thicker abdomen, which is pale underneath, and lays her eggs in the stems of water plants such as rushes and sedges.

Emerald Damselflies peak in numbers in late summer and are found at a wide range of shallow water bodies. Despite being relatively common, they have declined in number over recent decades.

Close relatives include the **Willow Emerald**, a fast-spreading species which is larger and has an entirely metallic green body in both sexes.

Common Blue Damselfly

A variety of small and dainty blue damselflies inhabit watery habitats across Britain. Subtle differences in appearance between species, coupled with the fact that males and females of the same species are seldom alike, and colouring varies with age, make identification challenging.

The **Common Blue Damselfly** lives up to its name as one of the most abundant and widespread of our damselflies. It is the benchmark species when trying to separate our blue damselflies.

This delicate damselfly has a thin, light blue abdomen marked with barcode-like bands of black.

A key distinguishing feature is that, behind the head, both sexes

have a broad stripe on either side of the top of the dark thorax. In other blue damselflies these pale 'shoulder' stripes are either thin or absent.

Male Common Blue Damselflies (*above*) flitting low over the water are noticeably bright blue in the sunshine. The tip of the tail has blue segments, which particularly stand out against the adjacent black banding. And near the top of the abdomen, just behind where the wings join the body, there is a small black mark shaped a bit like a mushroom (*left*).

Males actively pursue females and keep hold of them after mating, guarding against rivals while the female lays her eggs on plants growing at the water's surface.

Azure Damselfly

The **Azure Damselfly** is very similar-looking to the Common Blue Damselfly – the males being bright blue with black markings, while females are darker and often greenish. However, the Azure Damselfly has narrow, rather than thick, 'shoulder' stripes on the dark thorax.

The males of both species can also be told apart with a close-up view of the abdomen – perhaps using binoculars or a camera zoom lens. At the top of this tail section of the body, close to where the wings join the thorax, the male Azure Damselfly has a black 'U' shaped mark (*right*), whereas the male Common Blue Damselfly has a black mushroom shape in the same position.

Of these two widespread and common lookalikes, the Azure Damselfly is more likely to be found at small garden

Blue-tailed Damselfly

An abundant species of lowland water bodies, the male of this damselfly is aptly named, having a distinctive bright blue band near the tail end of its black abdomen.

The male's thorax has blue sides and narrow blue 'shoulder' stripes. The thorax and tail band of females vary in colour, with the palette of possibilities including purple, blue, olive and brown.

There are other species with which the **Blue-tailed Damselfly** could be confused. The most common of these is the male **Red-eyed Damselfly**. It shares the long, dark abdomen, tipped with blue, but has noticeably red eyes. Male Red-eyed Damselflies also lack the blue 'shoulder' stripes of male Blue-tailed Damselflies.

Female Common Blue Damselflies (*above*) have more black on their abdomens than males and some are greenish – their broad shoulder stripes in these cases being green, rather than blue.

The species is found across Britain in a wide range of freshwater habitats, including ponds and rivers. Despite its size, at less than 4cm long, it will fly out over open water, and large numbers can often be found around the margins of wetlands amid waterside reeds.

The tiny larvae eat live aquatic prey and moult regularly as they increase in size. Water temperature affects the length of time it takes the larvae to fully mature – one year in the southern part of the species' range, and two years in the north. The flying adults emerge between May and August, peaking in June.

ponds than the Common Blue Damselfly. But both species breed in a wide range of watery habitats in Britain.

Newly emerged damselflies are less intensely coloured than fully developed adults. They typically head off to feed and mature before returning to the hurly-burly of the waterside to breed.

Mature adult Azure Damselflies are often seen in summer joined together as they mate, flying 'in tandem' while the female deposits her eggs on aquatic vegetation in the shallow margins of water bodies.